YOUR
LIFE
MATTERS

Tips from America's Favorite
Teen & Family Life Coach

JEFF YALDEN

YOUR LIFE MATTERS

TAKE TIME TO THINK TIPS from Television's Favorite Teen & Family Life Coach, Jeff Yalden

Published by: BOOM Publishing
122 Pheasant Run Drive
Murrells Inlet, SC 29576
Email: Jeff@JeffYalden.com
Web: www.JeffYalden.com

Printed in the United States of America

ISBN: 197450283X
ISBN 13 Digits: 9781974502837
Your Life Matters (February 2013)

Warning – Disclaimer
The sole purpose of this book is to educate and entertain. There is no guarantee made by the author or the publisher that anyone following the ideas, tips, suggestions, techniques, or strategies will become successful. The author and publisher shall have neither liability nor responsibility to anyone with respect to any loss or damage caused, or alleged to be caused, directly or indirectly by the information contained in this book.

TOUCHING HEARTS...

" *This book reflects who Jeff is, and from personal experience, I can say that if you take the time to really feel the words Jeff has written, they have the potential to incredibly impact your life. This isn't a book you should want to read. It's one you really have to read.*"

— B. CASWELL

Student, Harvard University, Harvard, Mass.

" *Your Life Matters is an excellent road map to success. Every teen and even every adult should read this book. It is a true illustration of how to be successful in all aspects of life! A true reminder of the way things were, yet forgotten, and how they should be now! A wonderful learning tool!*"

— J. HAYES,

Director of Special Education, Hollis-Brookline High School, Hollis, N.H.

CHANGING LIVES

DEDICATION

To the hundreds of thousands of teens, teachers, parents, and communities I have had the pleasure of working with. You've inspired me and continue to inspire me every day. Enjoy the book. I hope our paths cross in the future.

To Janet, thank you for your uncondtional love and support as I continue to grow and learn every day. I love you!

TABLES OF CONTENTS

A MESSAGE FROM JEFF

Since 1992, I have worked with teens, youth, and families in different capacities, and I couldn't ask for a better career. Imagine, if you will, the satisfaction that comes from helping a young adult get on a path to success. You may have gotten a sense of what I do if you watch MTV's reality series "MADE" regularly. I was on an episode in late 2005. As the life coach on the show, I helped an 18-year-old high school senior find out what she was most passionate about so she could decide on a college major and career. She moved me as much I moved her. From teaching and coaching to speaking and mentoring, I have had the honor of reaching nearly four million youths and educators from all over North America and student leaders representing more than 48 different countries. It has been just awesome and rewarding, meaningful and fulfilling.

I love teens and how they keep it real. Within a heartbeat they'll read you and without hesitation tell you what they think and what they want and expect that success will be greeting them within a few years. While the dream to be successful is there, one major obstacle must be overcome. Somebody has to teach them the essential principles for achieving success or how to define what success or purpose means to them as productive members of a community within our society. Your Life Matters, this isn't just what I do. This is who I am!

In some cases I feel that we, as role models and mentors to young people, mislead them: Go to school, you'll learn to become successful. Although school is very important and plays a very significant role in one's success, I do believe there is more to living a life than just going to school. Education is a large piece of the puzzle in creating a successful life, but there are other pieces to that puzzle that are essential to reach professional and personal success.

The other pieces are included in what I call the STREETS of LIFE or the other side of EDUCATION. Certain skills that are important, such as respect, responsibility, setting goals, defining a purpose, managing money and time, choosing a career, overcoming obstacles, and making the right choices, are extremely important, not to mention attitude, role models, self-respect, and the wisdom of others. All of those ingredients build upon the educational foundation provided by an academic institution, whether it is middle school, high school, college or a university.

I have written this book based on my experiences working with MTV and more importantly, my passion for working with teens and youth. This book will offer advice, based on my opinion and experiences in life, and provide a road map for leading a purposeful and very successful life. More so than anything, this book teaches the essential principles for succeeding in the REAL WORLD and on the STREET.

I tell young people that success has already started for you the moment you were conceived. Think about it: One sperm raced against 500 million other sperm through a long tunnel for one egg. YOU WON! That means you are already successful. All you have to do now is capitalize on that success. Remember success begins to be more important to us as teenagers and continues to influence us for the rest of our lives. This is the time when we can put these key principles in motion and begin to create and shape our future.

This information I have written should be expected in every school and taught in every family to every child, preteen, or teen.

I have written it in a simple, easy-to-understand manner, in my language so you can easily understand the key elements of future success. I caution you that although this book is not difficult to read, it can and will be life-changing, so proceed carefully. Within these pages you will find some of the most valuable information that you will ever learn. This information builds on our educational experiences. If you read this book in its entirety, I am sure you will be going places, and other people will ask why they're not going, too.

The principles in this book have one objective:

TO GIVE YOU THE READER A PERSONAL COACH TO HELP PROVIDE A PATH FOR EXTREME PURPOSE AND PASSION IN YOUR LIFE THAT OTHER TEENS DON'T HAVE.

Are you ready? Then let's go!

CHAPTER ONE

YOU MUST THINK YOU CAN

First things first. You must understand that the outcome of your life is a result of your actions and behaviors. Your actions and behaviors come as a result of what you personally believe. What do you believe? Do you believe that mankind was a mistake created by a cosmic disruption in dual realities? Do you believe that fate is the direct result of karmic influences? No, wait. Let's not start off too deep here. What do you first believe about yourself? I used to always believe that I wasn't capable, that I wasn't smart enough, that I didn't have the ability, the capability, or the intelligence to do something significant in my life.

What you believe is what creates your actions and behaviors. Your actions and behaviors are what will determine the outcome you are seeking in life.

Belief - Behaviors - Outcome

"*The outcome of your life is directly influenced by your behaviors, and your behaviors are influenced by what you believe.*"

– JEFF YALDEN

I remember the early days of my life when I was told, "If you think you can make the shot, chances are you can make the shot. If you think you can pass the test, chances are you'll pass the test. If you think you can, you probably will, but if you think you can't, you probably won't." The lesson: If you think you can do something, chances are good that you will, but if you think you can't, you probably won't.

> *"You're only as gifted as the gift
> you think you posess."*
>
> – JEFF YALDEN

We become sabatoged by listening to others. Never let any outside influence have power over your own emotions. No matter what is said or done, it doesn't matter unless you are believing in what they are saying. Nobody else is living in your body, mind, and spirit; therefore, their words should have no effect on how you feel about yourself or what you want to do.

We all dream of what we want or where we will be or whatever we will accomplish, and that is great. However, if you don't first believe in the dream, then the dream won't become true. You must first believe, because belief will give you the behaviors necessary to accomplish the dream.

I will never forget when I was in the Marine Corps stationed at Cecil Field, Naval Air Station in Jacksonville, Florida. It was there when I truly realized the power of what you believe. If the belief is real and strong enough, then the outcome is more likely to be what you want.

I was going before the Meritorious Promotion Board to step up in rank. The four guys I was going up against all had at least one year's time in service ahead of me, but that didn't stop me from believing. They were more experienced, great guys, excellent Marines, well respected, and everyone thought I didn't have a chance because of the quality and experience of the competition I was going up against. But I believed in myself, and I knew my Marine Corps rules and regs better than anyone. I believed in my ability as a United States Marine. To me, it didn't matter what others thought or that the other Marines were more experienced. I believed in myself. I knew what I could do and what I could be!

Simply because I believed in myself, my behaviors changed. I did whatever it took to prepare myself for this one long day of interviews, tests, educational challenges, and whatever else was going to come my way. I was going to attack it because I was ready.

"I visualized where I wanted to be, what kind of player I wanted to become. I knew exactly where I wanted to go, and I focused on getting there."

– MICHAEL JORDAN

The day came, and I could not have been more ready. "Bring it on," I thought. "Prepare to win, and you'll win. Prepare to fail, and you'll fail." I was prepared and knew that I won before the day took its course. I was so confident that I had won that I even put a new sticker on my car that had my new rank. I was probably a little too confident, but I just knew it. I didn't have to remove that sticker!

"I had a dream and aligned my purpose in the direction of that dream regardless of what others believed. It came true."

– JEFF YALDEN

Dreaming is a great thing to do. I love to daydream, but let me ask you something. If you dream of what you want but don't believe you are capable of achieving those dreams, then what does the dream mean? Dreams give you the mental picture of the success you want in life but believing causes you to take the actions necessary to make your dreams come true. Dreaming allows you to visualize the outcome; actions make that outcome become real. For me, dreaming always gave me the vision of the future I desired.

That day the dream was alive and running through my body like water flushed through a toilet. That was the dream, but the belief was stronger than the dream itself. The dream is where it all starts, but the belief gives you the behaviors to accomplish what some might think is impossible. All that matters is that you believe.

The problem with dreaming is that most people think their dreams will never come true. This is because we don't first believe in ourselves or our ability.

I was one of those people once myself. But then one day I read in a book a quote that said, "You can do anything you put your mind to. If you can dream it, you can do it."

From that moment on, I never settled for anything less than my dreams. If I dreamed about achieving something, I pursued it until I had achieved it. Anything that I have ever accomplished in my life began with dreaming about it first.

Dreaming and believing that you will achieve your dream is half the battle. Once you are determined to achieve your dream nothing will stop you. Walt Disney once said, "All our dreams can come true – if we have the courage to pursue them."

That beautiful day ended with me winning unanimously and being selected as Corporal with only 19 months time in service. That was the fastest that anyone at Marine Corps Security Forces Atlantic had ever rose the ranks to Corporal. I became a Non-Commissioned Officer in the United States Marine Corps. Ooh-Rah . . . Semper Fi!

I followed the same belief when it came time for the Marine-of-the-Year board. I believed, and that is all that mattered. I prepared because I knew I had a chance. I was confident. When you believe in yourself, you are willing to do whatever it takes to reach your goals. You will then prepare as much as you can.

To prepare, I went back to Parris Island, South Carolina where my former drill instructors were. I drove the six hours to meet with them. I made sure my uniform was squared away and ready to roll. I made sure my military bearing was in tip-top shape and that I didn't lose any discipline. They drilled me across the entire range of my Marine Corps knowledge and told me at the end of the day that I was ready. I was! Bring it on!

Well, I won Marine of the Year (two years in a row). How do you like that?

"If You Can Dream It, You Can Do It!"

Please take the time to remember that simple phrase. Dreams are not difficult to fulfill. We only think they are difficult because most people are afraid to pursue their dreams. Be different. You have the ability to achieve anything you desire. Simply make the decision to turn your dream into a goal. Then pursue your goal until you achieve it.

Remember the most important point: You can't turn your dream into a goal if you don't first believe you can accomplish the dream. If you believe in yourself and change your behaviors/attitudes as a result of what you believe, you will accomplish what so many people, because of their fears, have never even tried to do.

Your success in life starts with the dream. To accomplish anything in life, you first must picture it in your mind, feel it in your heart, and desire it in your soul. Things are not achieved by chance. I will not disagree with luck playing a role at times, but to set out and accomplish something, you first must form a mental picture of how you would feel and what positive things will happen when you realize your dream.

All successful people dream, even some of the most popular people in the world. Their popularity didn't just happen. It came about because they believed in their ability to succeed and created the right mental image of their success.

No one has ever achieved anything great without first dreaming about it. Dreams form the mental picture of what we desire most in our life. The problem with dreaming is that most young people believe that their dreams can never be real. Or, they listen to those who tell them that they'll never achieve their dreams.

As you begin trying to accomplish certain goals in your life, you will meet people who will criticize you and try to bring you down. Stay away from these negative people. You don't need negative-thinking people in your life.

Don't worry about what others think. It only matters what you think and believe. Don't try to please all the people in your life, as that is the quickest way to fail and be miserable. To be the best you can be, you only have to please yourself.

If your friends do not support and encourage you, then they are not your true friends. True friends will believe in you and will help you figure out how to achieve your dreams.

Those who tell you that it can't be done are the very people who are afraid to pursue their own dreams. They are jealous of anyone who succeeds, because if you are moving forward and achieving goals in your life, then people will notice you and not notice them.

"Those who say it cannot be done should not interrupt those doing it."

– UNKNOWN

HAVE A POSITIVE ATTITUDE

"Attitude is like pee in your pants.
Everybody can see it, but only you can feel it."

– JEFF YALDEN

Gimme some attitude. No, I'm not talking about the show you put on when a parent tells you "no way" to a certain fragrance-maker's tee-shirt, the one that says "FCUK" (French Connection United Kingdom). I'm talking about a can-do attitude. Success or failure is built upon your attitude going into whatever you do. Attitude is the foundation that gives you the motivation to create all the ideas that are formed by your thoughts. What you focus on is what you become. Your negative thoughts and "I CAN'T" statements will hinder you and hurt your progression because it will create a negative belief in your own ability. The same for the "I CAN" statements. "I CAN" will motivate you to push through the tough times. "I CAN" will give you the belief that you are capable. "I CAN'T" will talk you out of any possible thoughts for success. All thoughts that you have will store in your brain housing group and your memory and you'll never forget them. That is why it is critical to have positive thoughts every day throughout every situation and circumstance.

If you continuously store negative thoughts in your brain, you will eventually become a negative person who seeks to be with other negative people wallowing in their own self pity thinking that life dealt them a bad set of cards. It may not be today, tomorrow, next week, next month, or next year. But be assured that one day it will happen to you. Change your attitude NOW.

Begin right here, right now, to make only positive statements and to think only positive thoughts. To get the results you desire in life, you must change your thoughts. What you focus on, you will achieve, because thoughts are transformed into actions, and actions produce results. If you change the way you think, then you can change the person you become. Anything that happens in life first begins as a thought. Make that statement positive by using "I CAN" and not "I CAN'T" statements. Like Nike says, "Just Do It."

Take your attitude to a new level, and you will take your success to a whole new level as well. Develop a strong mental attitude, and your chances of reaching your full potential are greater. Most people think negative thoughts rather than positive thoughts. It's simple – think positive thoughts if you want positive results.

Positive Thought + Positive Attitude = Positive Results

Negative Thought + Negative Attitude = Negative Results

Start right now to develop a positive attitude and begin focusing your thoughts on believing in yourself and your abilities. Before you realize it, you will be accomplishing things you once thought only great people accomplish. You are great, and you need to start thinking that way too.

What The Students Are Asking:

 What is the most positive way of getting a boost from yourself and your surroundings to give you encouragement to stand up and do better in life and in school?
- *Mubashir M., Ocean Township High School, NJ*

Answer: Your surroundings are your influence in life, both positive and negative. Surround yourself with like-minded people that are willing to work hard and ask the right questions. You want the best for your life? Then get involved, ask questions, read, do your homework, and seek the wisdom, experience, and knowledge of people that have walked before you. You have this attitude and surround yourself with those like-minded and you will do better in life and in school.

 What is the most rewarding experience you have had about speaking to schools?
- *Ryan Ross, Ocean Township High School, NJ*

Answer: The most rewarding experience I have had and I still have is that every night I lay my head on the pillow and I think of how fulfilling, rewarding, and meaningful my life is. I'm honored that my life has meaning and influence. I think there is no better reward.

 What is your favorite part about being a motivational speaker?
- *Cooper Nisbet, Quincy High School, IL*

Answer: My favorite part of being a motivational speaker is when people tell me they're motivational speakers too. Then in the conversation they allude to the church youth group they speak at and the boy scouts. I get a laugh. Seriously, I think that is my favorite part. Nobody knows the work I have put in to be where I am today – one of the Top 7% of Professional Speakers World-Wide. My second favorite part of being a motivational speaker is that I actually get paid for doing what I love. Awesome! Cha Ching!

CHAPTER TWO

YOUR ATTITUDE
IS EVERYTHING

Attitude is everything. I know you have heard that before. Well, believe it. Nothing can be as influential as your attitude.

Listen, I don't smile because I am happy. Happy people are not happy all the time. Happy people celebrate happy moments. I'm vey open about my mental illness. Yes, I live with mental illness. I smile because I am grateful and because I choose not to be a victim and make excuses.

Don't mistake this for the side-of-your-head-looking-like-it's-bouncing-off-the-side-of-a-wall-while-you-can't-keep-your-eye-on-your-dodging-finger-as-it-points-up attitude.

This is the attitude that controls the choices you make. You make poor choices when you have a negative attitude. You make good choices by having a positive attitude. Keep it simple. You have to take charge and control of your attitude every day. Nobody else can control your attitude. It's up to you. The best way to control your attitude is to understand some influential facts that help or hurt our self-esteem.

I can let depression rule me or I can figure out how to rule the depression. I will not submit to anything more influential than how I personally want to feel.

CREATE THE SELF-RESPECT YOU DESERVE

Many of us don't like ourselves and are constantly comparing ourselves to the people around us. We are looking for our identity and
the meaning of life from others. Unfortunately, we are looking in the
wrong places. To create a positive self-image we need to be happy
with ourselves. That can come only as a result of our commitment to
personal well-being.

It's easier said than done – I know. But when you have the right
self-image, your life will blossom and you will feel capable of growing
and succeeding. If you can't respect yourself, then you can't respect
others. If you can't respect others, then others will not respect you. If
you're not respected, then, of course, you'll be negative!

Self-image takes discipline, courage, and commitment. Having commitments in life is the best way to create oneself and to develop a purpose. Having a purpose in life is a key component in creating a positive
self-image. Having commitments gives purpose to your very existence.

---

*"The self is not, in essence, waiting to be
discovered. The self is, in essence, waiting to
be created."*

– DR. ANTHONY CAMPOLO

KNOW THAT YOU ARE SPECIAL

I love that quote and I love Dr. Anthony Campolo. You create the person you want to be and it doesn't matter what others think of this person that you are. It matters most what you think of YOU! Remember, "Your Life Matters" . . . YOU MATTER!

Think of it this way: At one time, you were a sperm. Yes, you were once a sperm. Little head. Squiggly tail. Always in a rush when the door opens. But you were not just any sperm. You were one of some 500,000 sperm. There was only one egg. Five hundred thousand sperm and one egg! All you sperm once lined up at the starting line. You raced each other down a long tunnel. In the end, YOU WON! Isn't that amazing? One egg, and you were the one among 500,000 sperm who won. The Olympics has nothing on you. You won the most important race ever!!! You are special and fast too!!

SELF-ESTEEM

Have you ever seen a relationship where a man treats the woman poorly? Do you know why that is? When the man doesn't think much of himself and doesn't believe in himself, he builds himself up by tearing down his spouse. Some men do that to show they are better by comparison. They build themselves up while tearing others down.

That is what I once did, and I am ashamed of it. Needless to say, my relationship with the woman I treated poorly ended in a divorce and significant pain.

At the time, I thought it was her fault, not mine. I didn't take personal responsibility for the situation at all. So I met another woman a short time later, and the same thing happened. I chose to build myself up by tearing her down. I wanted to show that I was better by comparison. Well, that relationship ended too, and I was to blame, although I still didn't take personal responsibility for my actions.

One day, though, I woke up and looked at myself in the mirror. I thought I was a loser. I decided to really look at myself. I didn't like whom I saw, didn't like whom I was, and didn't like what I was seeing down the road. I knew I had to make some changes. The first thing I did was start to improve my self-esteem and take personal responsibility for my life.

I speak mostly to ladies on this, but please any of you who are reading this, please, if you ever encounter a relationship like that, please get out and know that no man or no woman should ever treat their significant other this way. It is wrong, unhealthy and unacceptable behavior for any relationship. Your personal self-respect has to be greater than any person, place, or thing, and you must know that it is not the relationship you want to have. Love the skin you're in, and accept nothing better than what you expect and deserve in a relationship.

What The Students Are Asking:

 Should you ever regret something you did or didn't do?
- *Lukas M., Girard High School, IL*

Answer: I am sure we all live with regrets, but the questions is do you let it hold you back? Listen, I have regrets, but I think I am better of as a result of the lessons I've learned. We learn every day through experiences. The best experiences are the experiences someone else has lived and you have learned from them. Having said that, I don't think you should regret anything, but you should certainly learn from everything.

What made you feel courageous enough to share your whole story with so many people?
- *Della W., Jacobs High School, IL*

Answer: I never looked at it as courage to share my story. It was more that I had a story and I wanted to share so that others didn't have to think of themselves as I did when I was in school. I also live with wishing I had more self-esteem when I was young. I have regrets in my life as a result of the choices I made that were because I didn't think I was smart enough, fast enough, capable enough, etc. I wanted to teach you the greatest lessons I learned and my story was a way to keep it real and authentic.

You must like yourself before you can like someone else. You need to understand that. You can't seek a relationship thinking someone will make you happy. You need to make yourself happy first and then someone can compliment you and the self-respect you already have. You need to like yourself. Look in the mirror. Do you like whom you see? Who are you? Where are you going? Are you taking personal responsibility for your self-esteem?

FAILURE TEACHES SUCCESS

You will probably be like everyone and fail at something some time in your life. You will be in pursuit of accomplishing a dream when something holds you back. Your turn becomes an obstacle, a challenge, a course you did not want to pursue. You must understand that sometimes we do fail. Anyone who has become truly successful will tell you that their success didn't come easy. If success were easy, then everyone would be successful beyond his or her wildest imagination and I wouldn't be writing to you now. The important thing is that you never quit or give up when you fail.

Successful people are not afraid to fail. So what if you let it slip out that you're a vegetarian during the job interview at Taco Bell. Failure is a good teacher. Learn what you did wrong or what you have to do better to succeed next time. Failure is a part of trying. I would rather fail trying to accomplish something than never try at all. Don't quit when faced with failure; you may be closer to succeeding than you think.

Set your expectations higher than your friends and work hard toward them. Even if you fail or come up just short you will have learned valuable lessons that will serve you well for the rest of your life. You will also have accomplished more than the friends who didn't have any expectations or never tried to reach any dreams at all.

Thomas Edison failed about 2,000 times before finally inventing the light bulb. He didn't get discouraged. He didn't quit. He believed, which led to his behaviors. When he had an unsuccessful attempt, he would simply say that he was one step closer to finding the correct procedure.

Abraham Lincoln lost about eight elections before becoming President of the United States of America. Although he continued to lose elections, he never quit in pursuing his dreams.

Willy McGillicuddy – Do you know him? Exactly, because he quit in his dreams. Don't be a Willy!

Great accomplishments rarely occur on the first try. You will fail at some point. It's a part of life. Accept it, learn from it and get over it. Let it go. The way to overcome failure is to, first, realize that it happens, and then benefit from it. Failure will teach you valuable lessons about succeeding.

THE SCARE OF A LIFETIME

It was the Monday before Thanksgiving 2012. I had been on the road traveling and speaking for nearly six months. I lost track of my purpose during that time. I had money and time so I took advantage of a some of the things on my "Bucket List". I took off on the motorcycle and enjoyed some motorcycle vacations, great meals, and lots of sun and fun.

During this period I got away from exercising and working out. I need to exercise and workout because it helps my mood and depression. When I'm not working out and exercising, I like to eat and I am an emotional eater too.

So my schedule was going to slow down over the Holiday's and I thought about getting a physical. I was becoming scared of having a heart attach and dying while being on the road. I wanted to take a look at my health and know where I was. I knew my weight was getting up there, but I didn't think it was that bad.

I went in to see the doctor that Monday and had blood work done. Within three hours I received a phone call from the doctor asking me if I could come back in to see him immediately. That is never a good sign.

The next morning I showed up and sat down with the doctor for what I now call a "Coming to Jesus" talk. He looked at me and said, "Jeff, if you don't lose weight, you are going to die. You have diabetes, high blood pressure, high cholesterol, and sleep apnea (which I knew I had). Nevertheless, I was stunned. My weight had blown up to 340 lbs. I was tired. I was out of breath. The seatbelts on airplanes were becoming too tight and I already had bought an extender. Traveling was becoming painful and too hard. This was news I needed, a shock that I needed to make a change.

I consider this day the best day of my life. Hey, I've always been an athlete. I used to be an aerobic instructor and taught Step classes in New Hampshire. I love exercising, but I let it all get away. For what?

Here is the point of this story. Failure teaches success and so does becoming out of purpose with structure and routine. Self-esteem can only come from within, but when you lose sight of the little things in life that bring joy and happiness, then your self-esteem is effected.

I had to make a change immediately. I went home and said to my wife, "I'm going for a walk, would you go with me?" On that walk, I told my wife about the doctor's appointment and told her I was scared.

I got home, and I ordered P90X by Tony Horton. I was afraid I wouldn't be able to do it. Tony Horton says, "Push Play and forget the rest." That is what I did and am currently doing.

In a little more than a month, I have lost 25 lbs. I am walking 20 miles per week and monitoring what I eat with the smartphone app, My-FitnessPal. I have a long way to go, as I want to lose about 80 pounds.

The bottom line is that I am taking control of my life, and I want you to take control of your life. My life matters as much as your life matters, but when we look in the mirror we need to believe that our lives matter, and nothing is more important than the time we invest in ourselves being the person we want to be.

Your life matters! Make it matter and start today.

FIND ROLE MODELS AND EMULATE THEM

You are who you associate with. Associate with winners, you become a winner. Associate with losers, you become a loser. The person you associate with reflects the type of person you become. It just does! Find the positive people whose purpose and dreams are strong like yours and those are the people you want to associate with. Find like-minded people such as yourself and surround yourself with them every day and all the time.

Be a student of the game. Find people who have had the kind of happiness and success that you would like to have in your life, and then do everything you can to understand what they have done and emulate them. Learn what they are doing or what they have done, and then follow their path. Success leaves clues! Find the clues and incorporate them into your life. It's not hard, but you have to find these people and ask them the questions. They'll be happy to help you and answer your questions.

Find the qualities you like in other people and emulate them. Which of those qualities would you like to have? Write down these ideas, memorize them, and begin practicing them every day. Maybe start NOW! Soon, those qualities will become a habit, and they will become the qualities you use to describe yourself! Soon these great qualities will be the way others describe you too.

SEEK THE WISDOM OF OTHERS

I have learned in my life that birds teach birds how to fly, and fish teach fish how to swim. I have also learned that women need to teach young ladies what it means to become a woman. The same is true for the men in this world. Men need to teach young men what it means to become a man.

The problem is that in today's society, we are so caught up in our own lives. The busy schedules, the lost time, and the frequent interruptions prevent us from reaching all of our youths. That said, you need to take the time to seek out influences in life whom you trust and respect, whose opinions you value. Seek out their guidance, wisdom, and experience and don't ever be afraid to emulate them or ask them questions. You'll find out that they will be excited that you value them enough to seek their advice.

In my journey to regain the healthy lifestyle, I have started changing some influences. You might have to do the same thing too. It's ok. I now look for friends who are interested in exercising and walking. I spend less time with my motorcycle friends because I see that all they want to do is ride and eat. Riding is fun, but I can do that less and enjoy it more. Eating is fun too, but it also gave me the scare of a lifetime. Now, I need to focus on a healthy lifestyle, and I will seek those influences who have the same purpose.

It's been incredible working out to P90X with friends. My friends Bill and Eileen come every morning, and they bring their kids. It's been so much fun having support and encouragement as we build each other up.

TWO TYPES OF PEOPLE IN THE WORLD

You and I are one of two types of people in this world. No more, no less, but we are one of these two groups. Are you In-Purpose or are you Out-of-Purpose? Everyone in our society fits into one of these two groups. Which one are you?

If You Are In-Purpose...

You're unselfish. You recognize it is not about you, but it is about everyone. You have love in your heart and want to reach out and help other people without expecting anything in return.

If You Are Out-of-Purpose...

You are completely selfish. You think everything in life revolves around you. You want instant gratification; you want things right now and don't want to have to wait!

It is my hope that if you are reading this book, you are In-Purpose. Or, you are reading this book to become In-Purpose. Either way, I congratulate you; you are on the right track. You will succeed and win when you are In-Purpose and separate yourself from those in your life who may be Out-of-Purpose.

Listen, it is easy to live a life of being In-Purpose, but it's just as easy to fall Out-of-Purpose too. When you do, get back In-Purpose immediately. Find what works for you the best. This applies to your influences as well. When you feel like you are changing and don't like the person you are becoming, quickly look at who you are surrounding yourself with. Make changes immediately to live an abundant life of being In-Purpose. I guarantee you will like your life more.

EIGHT MOST POWERFUL PHRASES THAT BUILD INSTANT RESPECT

In today's society we have lost a lot of common respect for one another. Basic common courtesy has been put on the back burner or left out in the wind and blown away. If I can teach you nothing else but that, then this book was well worth writing. Here are the most powerful phrases that will take you places and earn you instant respect:

Please	Yes, sir	Excuse me	Yes, ma'am
Thank you	No, sir	You're welcome	No, ma'am

Those are simple phrases that show you are a person of character and class. If you were taught those phrases as a child, I compliment your parents and/or guardians. If you were not taught those phrases, then IT IS NO EXCUSE. Why can't you start using them today? Do not blame your lack of etiquette on others. It may be hard at first, but through everyday use, they become a part of you and will eventually come naturally. By using those phrases, people will look up to you and respect you for your maturity.

Here are some phrases that may not exactly take you places and earn you instant respect:

Chick	Aight	Kick it Phat.	Wazup!
Chill out, dude	Whatever	Da bomb	What's the

Another pet peeve of mine is the type of handshake in use today. Nowadays, I feel like I am shaking a dead fish when I meet someone for the first time. What is up with this? Where does this come from? Is a firm handshake being taught? Obviously not! Well let me tell you the right way to shake someone's hand.

First, you step into the handshake because it shows self-confidence and lets the other person know that you are not intimidated by the him or her. Second, you give a firm handshake; don't crush the bones in the other person's hand, but grasp the hand firmly. Then, look the person in the eye, as that builds trust and immediate respect. Be aware of how someone shakes your hand the next time. I bet you will see my point.

Another common courtesy I no longer see is holding the door for the next person. It used to be proper for a gentleman to hold the door for a lady. With the advent of equal rights it should be common for any person opening a door to hold it for the next person. So why isn't that true? It goes back to being In-Purpose or Out-of-Purpose. People who don't hold the door for the next person are Out-of-Purpose and only thinking about themselves. The next time you walk through a door, take a quick look behind you and hold the door with a smile. You will notice that being unselfish goes a long way; being In-Purpose gives you class and respect.

The use of common courtesy phrases, a firm handshake, and holding the door for others are easy, but often forgotten. Stop for a second and think about others, and use common courtesy in your everyday life. You will feel the change and reap the benefits.

AVOID NEGATIVE INFLUENCES

We are surrounded by negative influences everywhere we go. For example, we are influenced by the media all around us. Newspapers and televisions provide us with news and entertainment that enrich our daily lives. On the other hand, those same sources are filled with an abundance of gratuitous sex and violence. We as a society are surrounded by negative influences no matter where we turn. What can be done about that? There is a simple solution. The media and the entertainment industry are a part of our daily existence and will continue to be forever. How it influences us is our choice. We know what is positive and what is negative. Therefore, if we know that something is negative and doesn't benefit us, then we should turn ourselves away by not purchasing, watching, or partaking in it.

Another negative influence in our lives occurs when we choose the easy wrong over the hard right. Every day we are faced with choices that can, and will, determine the quality of our lives. That is why making positive choices is so important to our future success. Let me ask you this question, "Do you know the difference between right and wrong?" Every student I ask knows the difference, so I will assume that you know the difference as well. Therefore, when presented with a right or wrong situation, we should all be able to make the right choice. My point is that since we know the difference, then we should be expected to do the right thing regardless of whatever negative influences surround us.

Another negative influence is the lack of responsibility we are expected to take for our actions. Too many times in society I hear that we are trying to baby our youths in order to take the pressure of responsibility off of them. While that may seem like kindness, it is truly a disservice. Children who learn that they are not accountable for their actions tend to expect such treatment throughout their lives. When you make the wrong choice, you have to hold yourself accountable for it. You have to accept the consequences of your decisions. How does one grow up and become a mature member of society if he or she has not learned to accept responsibility? We need to be expected to make good choices and accept the consequences of our actions no matter what our age.

> **Remember:** *Avoid negative outside influences, make good choices, and take responsibility for your actions!*

You will encounter a time in your life when you are going to have to choose to upgrade the quality of influences in your life. Are you better off as a result of the people you hang out with or are you worse off as a result of them? You have to take personal responsibility as to whom your influences are. Who you associate with is who you become, and whom you become is a result of the people you associate with.

It takes courage to separate yourself from friends. However, you are the only one who knows if others bring you down or make you better. Here's a tip. Pay attention to what you are doing when you are out with your friends. Is it really what you feel you want to do? If it isn't, you're hanging out with the wrong people. Make the right choice, and do it now rather than later. You'll save yourself a lot of time in the future and many headaches.

Again, I need to reiterate the health scare that I am dealing with. It comes down to self-esteem, finding right influences, people in my life, being In-Purpose versus being Out-of-Purpose, trying to do too much, losing sight of my goals and dreams, etc.

Live your life in balance, and slow down and look at yourself in the mirror every day. Take time for yourself, and do the things that bring you a life of Purpose and Joy.

What The Students Are Asking:

 What can I do to avoid anger?
- *Luis A., Hubbard High School, IL*

Answer: The first person that is angry is always the first loser in any situation. Do what I do when I am angry. I ask, "Is this really worth being angry over?" I count to 10 before I respond. If 10 isn't long enough, I count to 100. If 100 isn't long enough, I go for a walk. Listen, "Anger is like Pee in your pants, every body can see it; but only YOU can feel it." Also, remember the 4 C's – Stay Cool, Calm, Collected, and always be in Control of your emotions.

 What was the hardest part of your life so far, and how did you overcome it?
– *Alexis W., Wellsboro Area High School, PA*

Answer: I think life is hard every day. I overcome it one day at a time and that is the truth. Seriously, I was a teen dad, I was in the hospital for depression, I had a negative self-image, I had a poor attitude, and on and on I can go. Stop feeling pity for yourself, circumstances, or situations. Get up and create something of yourself. Know that life and success is less about ability and intelligence, and more about attitude and choices.

Q If you could go back and change anything about your life, any of the not so great times, would you?
- *Brock L., Jim Thorpe Area High School, PA*

Answer: Probably years ago I would have wanted to change a few things. Today, I have to say, "No!" I am who I am today as a result of what I've been through both good and bad. The decisions and choices I've made have taught me a lot about life and me personally.

If I could change anything, maybe it would be people that I have hurt. Then again, today I know not to hurt and I am more compassionate and unselfish as a result. I think our lives are a culmination of everything we've been through and therefore, I am ok with what I've done, what I've been through, and who I am today as a result.

CHAPTER THREE

NEVER LOSE SIGHT OF THE FUNDAMENTALS

OK, so you want to be a photographer, let's say. You like taking pictures. So what's your aperture setting? "What-perture?" you ask? Nevermind. Next question: What's your f-stop? "F-stop?" you ask. "I'm still a virgin." Aperture and f-stops are fundamentals in photography.

Very often in music, theater productions, and sporting events, you'll see that the successful performers have mastered the fundamentals in their chosen field. Fundamentals are the basic ingredients for success. How can a basketball player be a star if he can't make a free throw or a lay-up? How can a great hitter continue to hit base hits every night if he doesn't first know how to see the ball and the type of pitch that is coming within that split second when he has to make a decision? Every professional was once a beginner. They had to learn the fundamentals before they were able to take their game to the next level, but at no point are they ever able to forget the building blocks that we call the fundamentals.

"Fundamentals are the key to your success in anything you do."

– UNKNOWN

Parris Island was where I went to boot camp as a United States Marine. It's a little island in South Carolina made famous by the Marines and many movies about it. The purpose of boot camp is to break down the recruits' previous habits and build them back up with the fundamentals developed by the United States Marine Corps standards.

We are creatures of habit, some good and some bad. That is exactly why boot camp lasts 12-13 weeks; it takes time to break the habits that have been a part of our lives for so long. It is when we can abandon our habits and form new ones that we learn to "unlearn" and develop anew.

Having said that, we need to look at life as a game and master the fundamentals in the game of life. We master the game of life by being fundamentally sound. Simple! Character, class, and unselfishness are the fundamentals of life and the basics of success and significance.

Greatest Lesson Learned in Character

Many people look at me after I speak and consider me their role model and write me telling me how great a man I am and that I am such a great person that has inspired them and changed their lives. I am truly honored and humbled by their kind words. Truly, I am, but I'm not perfect and I've made some mistakes that will stay with me forever. I accept that and I am proud of my past because the passion I have today is a result of having made some mistakes earlier on. The key is that every mistake I've made I have learned from. That is a good thing.

This next story is a mistake that cost me a dream, but taught me the greatest lesson ever. I'd rather learn the lesson than live the dream. Maybe you will understand after this story.

I served the United States Marine Corps with pride and honor. I wanted to be a career Marine and after my first tour I had put orders in to go to Parris Island and become a Drill Instructor. This was the dream of a lifetime. I wanted to become a Marine Corps Drill Instructor. My orders came back approved. On May 1, 1994 I was to report to DI School.

About three weeks before I was to report to Parris Island for DI School I was assigned Sergeant of the Guard duty on a Saturday. On Sunday, I was to be relieved by Sergeant Rushing. Sergeant Rushing was one of my fellow Non-Commissioned Officers who had nine years in the Marine Corps. He had a wife and three children. Good man. Good guy. We had served together in Japan and in the Gulf War. We had about 36 Marines in our Platoon.

Saturday went great. As the Sergeant of the Guard I was responsible for posting and relieving my Marines every four hours for 24 hours. Sunday morning at 9:00 am a new set of Marines would report and I'd be relieved by Sergeant Rushing. Come 0900 (let's be military here . . . .), Sergeant Rushing didn't report, but his Marines did.

What you learn in the military is that you don't leave your post until you are properly relieved. So, I stayed on post and took care of Sergeant Rushing's Marines. It was Sunday. I had no problem with this. As a matter of fact, this was the time when I was going through a divorce. Therefore, I had no money, but plenty of time. I was just fine with watching sports on TV and hanging out.

That morning about 1000, the Officer-of-the-Day had come by. He asked me where Sergeant Rushing was as he knew he was supposed to be in at 0900 with his Marines.

Here is my question . . . What would you have done? Would you have told the Officer-of-the-Day that Sergeant Rushing was no where to be found? That he didn't show up? Or, would you cover for your fellow NCO and lie to the Officer-of-the-Day?

Let me tell you about who this Officer-of-the-Day was. He had less than two weeks active duty in the United States Marine Corps. He just joined our Platoon. I didn't think he was in the need to know where a nine year veteran of the United States Marine Corps was. I'll put it this way . . . in the four years of my active duty, I had more time sitting on a toilet than this dude had active duty as a Marine. You're thinking TMI Jeff, huh? I know. Just trying to paint a picture . . . of the Officer-of-the-Day, not me on a toilet!

Let's revisit the question again. What would you have done? Oh, yeah, it was Sunday too. I mean, did I have to tell the truth when I didn't know where Sergeant Rushing was or what he was doing? It's ok to lie on Sunday's right? I'm sure you are thinking to yourself "Jeff, I would have covered for my fellow Marine. I'm not going to throw him under the bus."

I'll tell you what I did, I covered for him and said to the Officer-of-the-Day, "Hey Sir, yeah, Sergeant Rushing came but wanted to grab a bite at the chow hall. I was just hanging out so I told him I'd cover for him." I covered for Sergeant Rushing and lied to the Officer-of-the-Day. The Officer-of-the-Day said, "Oh good, have him come see me when he returns." I replied, "Yes, sir!" He walked away.

OK . . . I got away with that I thought. WOW! Sergeant Rushing never came around and I was at a loss because I was covering for him and didn't know where he was. I didn't have his number. We didn't have cell phones, instragram, facebook, twitter, or pinterest. I stayed on duty that day and later that afternoon the Officer-of-the-Day returned. "Corporal Yalden", he said, "Where is Sergeant Rushing?"

What would you do now? I'm already in the lie. Do I continue to cover up for him or do I tell the truth, but if I tell the truth now I am in trouble too. I couldn't rat our my fellow Marine because if I did the consequences could be costly. Lose rank, lose money. This would affect his family, kids, and his military service. I could put him in jail for being absent without leave . . . AWOL. What are you going to do? Make a decision. Be honest. Remember, it's Sunday!

I'll tell you what I did. Again, I covered for him and said, "Yes, Sir. He came back but needed a haircut and I was just hanging out." I lied again, but I needed to cover for my Marine. I can't rat out my Marine.

That Sunday night Sergeant Rushing showed up to the barracks. He was drunk and with another woman. She wasn't his wife. I knew that. I didn't say anything. I pretended that nothing was wrong. If he didn't know, then I wasn't saying a word. Remember, he was drunk and I wasn't going to try and reason with someone drunk. That doesn't make sense. Actually, it would make more sense being in the pool with Helen Keller playing Marco Polo than to try and reason with someone drunk. I left it alone.

The next morning, all the Marines arrive back to work. It was Monday about 0730 and I approached my Staff Sergeant. I told him the situation and asked for Friday off so I could enjoy a 72, which means 72 hours off, or three days off. I wanted a long weekend because I lost my whole weekend.

He replied that he would give me answer after the Monday morning meeting with all the brass. This included The Commanding Officer, Executive Officer, Staff Sergeants, Gunnery Sergeants, Warrant Officers, 1st Sergeant, and the Officer of the Day from that weekend. In the meeting, Staff Sergeant explained that I stood duty all weekend long and told them he'd be giving me Friday off. I was the Training NCO for all of 6th Marines at the time. It was necessary that he briefed everyone that I'd be off on Friday. He told of the situation. The Officer-of-the-Day was in that meeting when he heard the truth from Staff Sergeant. The Officer-of-the-Day then realized that I lied to him.

This ended my Marine Corps career. The Officer-of-the-Day wrote me up for lying to an Officer and lack of integrity. He canceled my orders to the Drill Field and denied my orders for reenlistment. Yes, on April 30, 1994 I was honorably discharged a United States Marine.

Do you think Sergeant Rushing is thinking of me today? How about the Officer-of-the-Day? Do you think that he would of covered for me like I did him?

Whose fault do you think this is? I mean, do you think the Officer-of-the-Day or Sergeant Rushing is a dumb dumb stupid head jerk? Probably!

Here is the reality. It is my fault. It is 100% ALL MY FAULT. Listen, I LIED. I chose to cover for him. Even on Sunday. I LIED and I AM 100% REPONSIBLE FOR MY ACTIONS AND CHOICES.

I'm proud to display my Dress Blues in my closet. I am proud to say I was a United States Marine and served honorably in the Corps.

Here is the moral of the story. You will find yourself in situations as you journey through life. You'll be put in a position where you have to tell the truth or you can cover up the truth by lying. What are you going to do? Here is the lesson I have learned and I will never make another mistake again.

Don't ever compromise your character as a person for that of anybody else. NEVER! You shouldn't have to lie for anyone. No friend, partner, business person, or anyone should ever ask you to cover or put you in such a position. We are all responsible for our own actions and choices. Sergeant Rushing didn't show up for whatever reason he had. That is his issue and not mine. Put the responsibility where it belongs. He made a choice and so did I, but I made the wrong choice. I should of taken care of myself and been truthful.

This was a painful, but great lesson that I learned. It's a lesson that I couldn't pay for, nor would any textbook teach me different.

Again, I am not perfect and I've made mistakes, but these mistakes have taught me valuable lessons to share every day with people. I hope you hear the lessons learned as I have lived them. I never claim to be perfect nor will I ever. I do care and want you to not make the mistakes I've made. Do the difficult right over the easy wrong every time.

BE A PERSON OF CHARACTER

Now I suppose you could go around wearing a clown nose when you eat cafeteria food if you wanted to become a character. To have character is different. Character comes out in the dark; it's what you would do if you knew that you would never be found out. Think about it. How would you react to a situation if you knew you would never be found out? How you answer is a true test of your character. As simple as it sounds, in the long run, being a person of character helps you maintain a good attitude. You don't have to put on a mask, nor do you have to constantly be on the lookout. Why? You aren't living a lie. Being a person of character gives you the freedom to enjoy life without hiding anything. A person of character always wins in the long run.

"Be more concerned with your character than your reputation, because your character is who you are, while your reputation is merely what other people think you are."

– JOHN WOODEN

My brother is someone whom I really admire. He used to be a top Special Agent with the United States Secret Service. I call him Robocop. He traveled aboard Air Force One with President Clinton, President Bush Jr., and President Barack Obama. It's a big job with lots of stress but great stories to tell. Being a Secret Service Agent requires a person to be of good moral character. Today, he does CSI work for the United States Army and lives in Germany. Yeah, he does Top Secret work, but his moral character has given him these incredible opportunities.

Before becoming a Secret Service Agent, my brother spent some time at the Naval Academy's Preparatory School in Bristol, Rhode Island. It was there that he learned about character. He passed his military experiences onto me, his younger brother. I think he thought it would be funny to treat me the way he was treated at the academy. I didn't think having him home was fun at all.

When my brother was home, it was my duty to wake him at 0645. Because he was about 6'7" and weighed close to 270, there was not much I could do to refuse his request. By 0700, I had to have his breakfast prepared and ready for him. At 0710, I had to clear the table and immediately report to the front foyer of our house, where I had to "push the ground" to the tune of about 100 push-ups at his command. He thought it was funny that he didn't get tired when I pushed. Then, at about 0740, I would have to rebound 100 free throws for him. Yeah, that was great! And all that before the bus would come to take me to school.

Oftentimes, my brother would serve as my babysitter. On those occasions he had more time to discipline me. One night, my parents went out and left us alone. As my parents drove out of the driveway, my brother threw me in the closet. A few days later (it was only a few minutes but seemed like a few days), my brother returned, and he asked me, "Jeff, what do you see in there?" I was in tears and didn't think he was very funny. I replied, "Rob, this isn't funny. Let me out. It's dark. I don't see anything. I do feel a lot of coats around here though." He said, "Jeff, I am going to teach you one of the most important lessons you will ever learn." He paused, and then said, "Jeff, what you see is your character." I was mad at him for locking me in the closet, but I can honestly say he made me understand what character is really all about.

I am thankful today for what my brother taught me. A lot of my successes today are a result of listening to my brother. Perhaps that is one of the reasons I say we should always listen to those older than us because they might have something valuable to teach us. I speak about character during my programs, but sometimes the best examples are illustrated by the words of others around me. A few years ago, I met a great gentleman in Jefferson, Ohio, when I was speaking at the schools there. His name was Don Lee, and when we were talking about character, he said:

"Your character is the only thing that walks back from the grave."

– DON LEE, ASHTABULA, OHIO

How true! People will never remember the car you drove, the house you lived in, or the size of your bank account. What they will remember and reflect upon will be how you lived your life and what kind of person you were.

Most things in life are material but your character is the foundation of your life and will outlast them all. Know your character, and be yourself; be who you are in the dark.

IF YOU WANT TO BUILD CHARACTER:	IF YOU WANT TO TEAR DOWN CHARACTER:
Help others	Call people names
Stay on task	Break rules
Tell the truth	Be irresponsible
Show respect	Hurt others
Be fair	Be selfish
Be honest	Get even
Follow rules	Be lazy
Be responsible	Give up
Show kindness	Tell lies
Do the right thing	Don't try your best
Have a good work ethic	Steal

I'll tell you another awesome story of character. I think all athletes seeking college scholarships should hear this story. My brother was an All-American in high school and was highly recruited to play college basketball. One of the coaches that recruited my brother was Bob Knight, then the coach at Indiana University.

Bob Knight, like all coaches, sent letters and made visits and phone calls. They all made their pitch, but Bob Knight stood out in one particular way.

It was at the Nike All-American camp. Bob Knight showed up and left after lunchtime. My parents asked Bob Knight why he was there for such short time and why he didn't stay to watch my brother play. His reply? I will never forget his words . . .

"I know he can play. That is why I am recruiting him, but I wanted to see how he handled himself with other athletes in the cafeteria. At this point, I am more concerned with his character than his ability to play basketball."

Character matters to college coaches when the school is interested in paying for your education. Character counts in life.

Next time you go to post something on Facebook, Twitter, or Instagram, remember who might be looking at what you post because they are making buying decisions about you at that moment.

Performance Enhancing Drugs & Professional Athletes Today

I am quite disturbed right now with professional sports. Performance Enhancing Drugs (PED's) have been rampant and athletes are doing anything to get the compeititve edge over others. Athletes have denied, denied, and denied and then they get caught or retire and they then admit to having used PED's. As I write this, today, Lance Armstrong has apologized to the "Livestrong Foundation." He shared his message to the world on Oprah and asked for forgiveness.

To me, it isn't that he used PED's that bothers me. He's certainly not the only one. What bothers me is that he LIED . . . HE LIED! A person of Character wouldn't lie and continuing lying. Tell the truth and be honest with yourself.

A Valuable Lesson in Character

Let me share with you a story that nearly destroyed my career and my life. Many years ago, I wanted to be the best speaker in the world. I wanted to be funny. I wanted to be the best. As I watched other speakers on the platform, I enjoyed so much watching and listening to others that I didn't think I was nearly as good as others I watched.

One speaker in particular, Mr. Mark Sharenbroich, whom I think is probably the best speaker in the world. He's funny and down right moving. He shared a story about a crayon that I liked.

I started using that story. I started by using a piece of it. Then I started using more of it. I started to make that story a part of my talk and I did it for quite some time. Maybe a year or so. I'll never forget the time when Mark called me.

I was in Rapid City, South Dakota at the airport when he called and went off on me. Listen, this is one thing that the National Speakers Association and all Professional Speakers frown upon. You don't share anyone else's stories and use them as your own. Many people do and although few may get caught, it is a lack of character and integrity. Anyways, I was crushed. I know what I did was wrong and immoral. I have many regrets and have since made up with Mark and asked for his forgiveness.

As a result of this I have lost the respect of a lot of people. Although this happened back in about 2002-2003, I still have Professional Speakers that won't talk to me or trust me. I lost a lot of friends and respect.

I'll share with you two things I am proud of as a result of this lesson:

1. I owned up to it right away and accepted the consequences and never ran. I am proud of that.
2. Right away, I said that if I was going to be successful as a speaker then I need to tell my story and not concern myself with being funny or the best. Tell my story and be the best me that I can be.

The reality is that I am a much better speaker today than I ever have been. I am more comfortable telling my story and not trying to be anyone else.

Mark, my apologies again and again . . . I am truly sorry!

People are comfortable with people who have class because the people who have class are comfortable with themselves. People of class don't run scared, they don't make excuses, and they don't hide. Most importantly, people of class don't build themselves up by tearing others down. People of class have respect for all and fear of none.

Like character, class is important to maintain the right attitude and fundamentals. A person of class is empathetic and compassionate to others. So, a person of class makes a great leader because he or she can instantly be trusted and respected.

"Criticism is the autobiography on oneself."

– JAMES RUSSELL LOWELL

One example of a class act is Coach Mike Kryziewski, the head coach of Duke University basketball. He is a man who exemplifies class, character, and what all leaders should be like. He is one of the most respected people in all of college basketball because of whom he is as a person, as demonstrated in the following story.

It was March 29, 1999, and the NCAA Division I National Championship of college basketball had just ended. Duke University had just lost to the University of Connecticut. It was an upset in college basketball because Duke was favored to win. After the game, Coach Kryziewski was interviewed. You would expect that a coach of a losing team would be discouraged, furious, and very upset. But, in typical Coach Kryziewski fashion, he stood there in front of cameras, newspaper reporters, and the entire world of sports with a smile on his face. When asked how he felt to lose to Connecticut, he stood there with grace, poise, and a smile on his face and said something I will never forget: "I can't be sad. I can't. I don't coach for winning games; I coach for relationships."

Wow! This is one of the greatest coaches of the game. For him to say it's not about wins and losses but about relationships exemplifies good character. That man said it all. It is about the relationships. Now that is class. Unselfishness is where people think about others before thinking about themselves.

People have more respect for you when they know that you are a person who truly cares about others. My life became more significant when I stopped thinking so much about myself and started thinking about other people. For me, it was hard because I had always been selfish. When I started to see the benefits of being unselfish, I became more successful, more income started to come my way, my quality of life changed, and, most important, my overall happiness increased.

What The Students Are Asking:

 If there was one life lesson you consider most valuable, what would it be? How did you learn this lesson and how have you been able to apply it to your life?

- Jacque M., Jacobs High School, IL

Answer: There are so many life lessons I've learned along the way, but I think one of the ones I don't emphasize enough in this book is simply what I thought when I was growing up. I thought our lives came down to intelligence and ability. I'm not gifted with either, but as I write this I have come to learn that my greatest achievements in life are a result of my choices and my attitude. I apply this to my every day life by exercising the 4T's – Take Time To Think in my choices every day. I also rely on my attitude every day in waking up and going through things I don't want to have to deal with. Suffering from depression and anxiety, attitude is big . . . HUGE! My choices and my attitude are the greatest gifts I've been given.

Q What inspired you to become an inspirational/motivational speaker?

- Brandon S., Mahwah High School, NJ

Answer: I try and speak to teens in a way in which I wish someone had come and spoken to me. That being said, what inspired me to become a motivational speaker was my past and how I felt about myself. I felt inadequate and incapable of doing anything or believing in myself. The inspiration was to reach out to teens of today and share with them my story, but also what I have learned. I'll be honest, never in a million years or dreams did I ever think 20 years later I'd still be speaking and speaking at the level of success I've achieved. This is just a dream and a privilege.

CHAPTER FOUR

HAVE COMMITMENTS IN LIFE

I am a committed individual. And it's not because of those voices I hear in my head that keep telling me, "Eat Kentucky Fried Chicken. Eat Kentucky Fried Chicken." Wrong kind of committed. The following three simple rules by which I live have become my commitments in life:

Rule #1 Do What Is Right

Rule #2 Do the Best You Can

Rule #3 Treat Others the Way You Would Want Them to Treat You

That is it. Listen, I don't even think I'm smart enough to make my own commitments. These rules come from a person I've admired and looked up to for many years. Mr. Lou Holtz, former football coach at the University of Notre Dame. I've adopted them as my rules as a result of hearing him talk about them. Made sense to me, therefore, I adopted them as the rules in which I will live my life. I'll explain more about Lou Holtz in a little bit.

I try not to complicate things, so everything I do lies within those parameters which I have set as commitments for myself. Our commitments in life create our identity. I would like to outline those three rules, as they have become the cornerstones of my success.

TAKE PERSONAL RESPONSIBILITY

I wrecked my dad's car when I was a junior in high school. He made me pay for the damages. Two weeks later I wrecked his other car, and he made me pay for those damages as well. I started my life about $13,000 in debt. However, I learned a great lesson as a result of that.

One night my mother shared this with me, and I will never forget her words. My mother said to me, "Son, when you are ready and willing to accept responsibility for the circumstances, conditions, behaviors, and most importantly for the choices of your life, it will be then and only then that you will have the power to change your future."

Wow! Those are words I will never forget.

I grew up and didn't take responsibility for my life. I didn't care to. I didn't take responsibility for my attitude, my grades, and my life. I just didn't.

Well, that came back to hurt me, but also, helped to make me who I am today. I am grateful for what happened because it is who I am, and without that happening I don't think I would be half the man I am today.

At 18 years old, I graduated from high school without plans for anything else. I didn't choose to go to one of the three colleges (out of 19) that accepted me. I was in a relationship, and she was my everything (so I thought).

I chose to join the Marine Corps, and that was a blessing in my life. I continued dating this one woman, who later became my wife and the mother of my two daughters, whom I dedicate this book to.

I learned that no matter what happens in life, we have to first take the responsibility for all circumstances, conditions, actions, etc. Only when we take responsibility can we make a change and take action.

Years ago, while going through some challenges and being hospitalized for depression, my grandmother asked me to listen to a tape. It was that tape by Lou Holtz (at the time he was the head football coach of the University of Notre Dame) that changed my life. My career today is also a result of that very same tape and the influence of Lou Holtz.

I wish more parents, teachers, and coaches would hold kids responsible for their actions. I guarantee you will learn quickly as a result of being help responsible.

Rule #1 – Do What Is Right

We know the difference between right and wrong; therefore, we should do what's right and avoid what's wrong. When you do something wrong, you need to understand and accept the fact that you are accountable for your actions and be willing and ready to be held responsible. You can avoid it by simply doing the difficult right over the easy wrong.

You will encounter times in your life when you have to go against what makes you happy in order to do the right thing. That is called RIGHTEOUSNESS OVER HAPPINESS. Sometimes being mature helps you to make good choices in your life.

THE "TAKE TIME TO THINK" WRISTBAND

I have these grey wristbands that say "TAKE TIME TO THINK." I love them, and they sell out almost everywhere I go. I got the idea growing up from my brother, and it was also something the Marines always said to us. My brother used to always say to me, "Jeff, stop and THINK before you act." Therefore, I tell young people to "TAKE TIME TO THINK" before they make decisions and before they start their day.

When making choices in life, you need to remember "TAKE TIME TO THINK" and how that little mantra can benefit you.

Did you know that 80 percent of Fortune 500 CEOs wake up an hour early every day to take time to think about their day? They prepare for their meetings, what's ahead for them, what circumstances they will encounter, people they need to talk to or see, etc. What do you do? Do you take time for yourself every day to prepare and think about what you need to do? Go ahead now, "TAKE TIME TO THINK."

Rule #2 – Do the Best YOU Can

The key word in this rule is YOU. It's about you, not someone else. Be selfish here, and do your very best in whatever it may be.

Many people believe that the average person is basically lazy and wants everything handed to him or her. I agree. I have found in my own experience that most people don't want to have to work hard or extend themselves. That attitude concerns me, because we are in an era where too many people want things without having to work for them. If you are lazy and unwilling to have to work hard, then what success can you achieve? No one will hand you success if you are unwilling to work for it yourself.

So, the question remains, "Do you want success?" Well then, be ready to work for it! One of the reasons why I am where I am today is because of my work ethic.

I heard Michael Jordan on television one time and while being interviewed, the question was asked to him, "Why are you the greatest basketball player ever?" His answer was this. "I must demand more of myself than anybody else demands of me! I want to be the BEST! Priceless words from one of the greatest athletes of our time. Work hard, push yourself, demand greatness of yourself and your abilities, and accept nothing less than the very best from yourself. Only then will you reap the rewards of your work.

When you do the best YOU can, nobody can expect anything more of you. In the classroom, out of the classroom, on the athletic field, off the athletic field, in a part-time job, or in any activity that you are participating in, just do your very best, and you will be a winner. I don't mean that you will always win the game, but I do mean that you will feel that you have won within yourself. Whether you win or lose is not important, but being proud of your accomplishments and how you played are fundamental to your commitment to excellence. If you are doing your best, then people will know you have a commitment to excellence.

Rule #3 – Treat Others the Way You Would Want Them to Treat You

I learned the importance of putting yourself first because of the health scare that I had. I am suddenly realizing that if I don't look out for me #1, I might not have much time left to continue being a husband, father, teen coach, speaker, or business owner. Take care of your mind, body, and spirit. I'll be stronger and ready for everything that lies ahead because I put myself first. We matter!

Do unto others as you would have done to you. Basically, treat and respect others the same way you would want others to treat and respect you.

I live my life simply by this: I don't care if you are black, white, Jewish, Protestant, Catholic, Christian, Muslim, Hindu, male, female, straight, or gay. I don't care if you drive a BMW, a Honda Accord, or a John Deere Tractor. I feel that we are all one, and nobody is any better than anybody else.

Wouldn't it be great if everyone lived by that rule? Then we would be without hate, prejudice, crime, and violence. We'd all get along much better. Life would be great.

The golden rule is so powerful and so meaningful. Why can't we be more helpful to others instead of hurtful? Why can't we all have more love in our hearts than hate in our souls? Where does true equality begin? It begins with us. We need to accept that people are born a certain way and make choices that are beyond our control.

For example, does a black baby, a white baby, a Jewish infant, or Catholic infant, perhaps even a person who is gay, have any say or choice in how they were born? People don't choose the circumstances of their birth, but we can all make the choice to accept other people for whom they are.

Make the right choice. I challenge you to make the first move to respect all people each and every day, one person at a time. And it starts here with you reading this. Now go out there and have a little more respect, a little more love, a little more understanding, and a little more compassion and empathy toward others.

I'd like to share with you a personal story that affected my life in many ways. Little did I know that my life would change as a result of what I experienced. I don't wish what I went through on anyone, but the experience has taught me much.

February 26, 1992
Cecil Field Naval Air Station, Jacksonville, FL

He was one of my Marines who chose to show up late back from a four-day weekend that we call a 96 in the Marines. It means 96 hours away. His name was PFC Eisenburg, one of my Marines at Cecil Field Naval Air Station in Jacksonville, Fla., from December 1990 to January of 1993. I remember PFC Eisenburg very well because he was always by himself and didn't really have too many friends. His uniform was never pressed, and his boots never really shined. He may not have been the best Marine, but he was one of our Marines.

The morning of February 25, 1992, PFC Eisenburg showed up late for duty and missed formation. As a disciplinary punishment, I put him on a 24- hour post. It was my responsibility to ensure that he was armed and on duty at all times. At 0400 on the morning of February 26, I got up to see how Eisenburg was doing. We talked for several hours as he shared with me a lot about his past and current life. He was down and depressed and shared with me that his fiancée of five years had just ended their relationship. Also, he told me his mother had left him when he was young, his father was in jail for drugs, and he hadn't seen his brother for about three years. Hours passed as we had a meaningful conversation.

At about 0730, he showed me a picture of himself, his fiancée, and his brother. After a few minutes of reflection, he dropped the picture at my feet and walked off in tears to his room down the hall. After a few minutes, I walked to his room. As I approached the room, I noticed that the door was slightly ajar. I pushed it open, and Eisenburg was sitting in his chair with a 9mm handgun at his chin, ready to take his own life. Careful of my every move, I looked at him, maintaining my sharp military bearing, and said, "Eisenburg, don't do it." He looked at me and said, "Nobody cares about me." I replied, "I care," and he said, "Maybe you're the only one."

You see, he wasn't a very good Marine, but that didn't make him a bad person. People just didn't give him a chance. Some were too quick to make comments or certain gestures toward him, and some just ignored him. That really affected him, and nobody really knew how he felt. I was standing about four or five feet away from him, desperate to find something to say that would be meaningful. I wanted so badly to jump across the room and knock the gun out of his hands. But I tried to be patient and talk him out of pulling the trigger and taking his own life.

At exactly 0738, on February 26, 1992, as I looked Eisenburg in the eye and he looked at me, his last words were, "Maybe you're the only one." He pulled the trigger as I stood there in front of him. As people arrived to help, I knew he was already dead. Did I fail in saving him? My answer is, "No."

I wish he hadn't died, but I am secure in the fact that I did everything I could at the time. His decision was already made before I entered the room. At least I got to tell him I cared before he died. I still miss him.

UNSELFISHNESS

*"One of the biggest questions
people will always ask about you is –
Do you care about me?"*

– LOU HOLTZ

One of the reasons I speak so heavily on the topic of unselfishness and caring is simply because of that story. I hope that because I shared with you that tragic day in my life, you will open up and care a little more about people.

We've seen lots of stories in the news lately about students wanting to kill other students or take their own lives because they feel they were picked on. That would stop if we could all do our part to stop hurting others and start helping instead. I hope that you can honestly say that you have never been the cause of someone else's pain. There is a great word in our vocabulary: HEART. In order to have HEART, we need to show we care. Within the word HEART is another word: HEAR.

We care through listening which also gives us the word EAR. There is a reason why we have two EARS and only one mouth; maybe we should use them in that ratio. We should listen two times more than we talk. Listening can make all the difference in the world when someone is in pain because then they know you care.

> **Quick question:** *Are you as beautiful on the inside as you are on the outside? Do you realize how many people have trouble answering that question?*

What The Students Are Asking:

 I know how much you enjoy traveling and speaking to different schools all around the United States, but how does your family deal with you always being gone?
- *Brooke S., Decatur High School, IL*

Answer: Sometimes my wife asks, "When are you leaving again?" This is all we've known. My wife is a teacher and she does her job extremely well. I am a motivational speaker and I like to think I do my job extremely well. We both come from hard working families that have created success for themselves. This is what I do and this affords us an opportunity to live the lives we live. Therefore, I hope that our work ethic is more important than our selfishness. Work hard and provide comes before anything else. I think my family deals pretty well because we are all hard workers and I am very proud of that.

When you are traveling to all these schools or events where you speak and you are away from home for a while, what keeps you going?

- *Owen J., Burnt Hills Ballston Lake High School, NY*

Answer: I think there are a few things that keep me going. For one, I love what I do and I am very grateful for this opportunity. I think another thing that keeps me going is simply knowing that I relate and share a message that teens enjoy listening to. I am not sure I am capable of doing anything else that I would enjoy as much as I enjoy speaking to teens. I love what I do and I love having created this business that gets to employ others and give people jobs. Think about it . . . I share a message about things I've learned that turns into income and opportunity. This is my life and I am blessed and honored. Love it.

CHAPTER FIVE

SAY NO
TO DRUGS

"I've never heard anyone stand before an audience and say, 'I am successful today because of drugs and alcohol."

– JEFF YALDEN

Recently, I spent a day with the Drug Czar in Washington D.C. during the PRIDE World Drug Free Conference. We spoke about the use of alcohol and drugs among youths today. His comment was that we were at an all-time low with the use of drugs and alcohol. I enjoyed hearing those comments. However, I was left to ask why is it so heavily mentioned in the media. After all, when we publicize something, it makes it more popular.

I personally don't think that drugs and/or alcohol are THE problem. Is it a problem? It's an issue, but here is THE problem: Students feeling the need to be accepted.

Today's youths have so many more opportunities than we had twenty years ago. Think about it. With technology today, youths have more access to gain knowledge and find information; they also have more pressure to perform.

Trying to keep up in a constantly demanding world, our youths feel the need to be accepted by others and do what others are doing so that they will easily be accepted by them. It's not the drugs, the alcohol or the smoking that's cool; it's the people doing these things who our teenagers think are cool. So to fit in, they join in. When a person's self-esteem is not where it should be, then the person feels the need to be accepted, and he or she will do anything that is perceived as "cool."

Therefore, having said that, you need not feel the need to be accepted; rather you need to first learn to accept yourself and not be so caught up in what others think.

MAKE THE RIGHT CHOICES

Every minute of every day you make a decision. You are constantly making choices. Consider these, for instance: Would you choose to be locked in that jail cell with an inmate who keeps scratching the chest of his thinning, stained sweatshirt, a collection of gnats floating about, or would you choose to have the keys to a red Porsche convertible? So those are extreme choices. Still, you choose what time to get up, what time to go to bed, what to wear, what to eat, who to talk to, who not to talk to, to do your homework or not to do your homework. You choose whether you are going to be on time or you are going to be late. You choose whether you are going to commit to giving your best effort.

Decisions are so powerful. Each and every decision you make every day will shape and define your future. Making one wrong choice can change your life forever. The problem with making decisions is most people think, "It will never happen to me!" It can happen to you, whatever "it" may be.

Labor Day weekend 2003 was an awesome weekend just like any other Labor Day I have lived before. This one was slightly different, though.

One of my former student leaders at a local high school where I live was a great girl with a great future. I will say her name is Suzy. Some people say that what happened wasn't her fault, but that a simple choice could have prevented her death.

It was late Friday night about 1:00 a.m. when Suzy was with her boyfriend – I'll call him Sam – and two other students at a local Dunkin' Donuts. They were drinking and having a good time. Suzy wasn't drinking alcohol, and there was no alcohol in the car. However, the other kids were drinking that night.

As the night wore on, Suzy and Sam were racing home along a major route where the speed limit is 45 miles per hour. It's a winding road that travels alongside the river up into the mountains. "Sam" was driving about 80-90 miles per hour in a 45-miles-per-hour zone. The choice here is that Suzy could have chosen not to get into the car, knowing that Sam had been drinking. However, she chose to go home and chose to buckle up.

The attitude that "it will never happen to me, we'll be fine, everything will be cool, we'll make it home, no problem" got the best of all of them. Sam lost control of his Honda Accord while going around a bend. The car hit the guardrail, hit the rock wall, spun a few times, and

flipped over a couple of times. They were all alive and OK. Thankful-
ly, they were wearing their seat belts. The second choice here is that
Suzy could have told him to slow down. Perhaps she did, but he didn't.
I don't know.

What I do know is that there was another car that night at Dunkin'
Donuts. A 24-year-old guy, who had just purchased a brand-new Ford
Mustang, was with a few other students from another high school.

They too were racing that night on the way home. They too were
doing about 80-90 miles per hour; however, they didn't see the car in
the middle of the road. As they came around the corner where Suzy
and Sam's car had flipped over in the middle of the road, they hit it.

The end result is that Labor Day weekend when people were supposed to be enjoying one of the final weekends on the boat, having fun,
and enjoying the weather, the people of this local school were gathe-
red at the high school mourning the loss of a great student whom they
will never forget.

You see, that car coming up the road didn't see the flipped car, and
it collided right into the passenger's side door where Suzy was sitting
with her seat belt on.

Raise your self-esteem, love yourself, and believe in yourself. Be selfish here for a second. You don't need to be accepted by others. You
have to accept yourself. When you do that, others will feel the need to
be accepted by you.

You know that drugs and alcohol are not good for you and are il-
legal. I will never say DON'T do drugs or drink. You have heard that

1,000 times before. Instead, make good choices and know that no drug or drink will ever make you happy with yourself or with your career. Drugs and alcohol will never help you get ahead. They will only hurt you.

The choice is yours, but here is some help to understand further: What do you think you possibly gain from using drugs? They cause people to self-destruct, families to be ruined and broken up, and careers to be destroyed. As a time bomb will explode, so will your mind, body, and your life, if you choose to be friends with drugs.

You can't tell me that drugs are cool and that everyone is taking them. Everyone is not taking them. How cool do you think it would be if drugs got you kicked out of school? Then you'd have difficulty getting into college. You say, "I'm not going to college." Therefore, you think it won't matter. Well, the military won't take you either. Once you get that negative mark on your "Life Report Card" for messing with drugs, you can't erase it. But you can turn your life around. If you're messing with drugs, simply MAKE THE RIGHT CHOICE TODAY and stop.

If you make a mistake in life and choose to turn your life around, please write to me and tell me about it. I'll be happy for you. Nobody is perfect, but it takes heart, courage, character, and class to turn your life around. That to me is a successful person who wants to succeed.

Do you think you will be cool if you mess with drugs and jump out of a window because you think you can fly? It happens.

Drugs can cause you to do things that you normally wouldn't do. They may cause you to hurt or even kill someone. They can even kill you. Do you want to take the chance of dying just to get a cheap high? Yes! Suzie was killed instantly.

THINK BEFORE YOU DO DRUGS

You shouldn't need drugs to get high. You should be high on life. The high should come from your friends, hobbies, sports, theater, music, extra curricular activities, etc. The challenge of doing your best and succeeding, seeing the results from your hard work in school should give you the high you need. It is the positive things in life that can give you so much more of a high than any drug ever can give you. Drugs don't help you enjoy your life; you help you enjoy your life.

I can write everything in this book, but still only you can make the choice. I personally have never in my life ever picked up a cigarette. I didn't drink in high school, didn't drink in the Marine Corps, and don't drink now. I just never have. It never appealed to me, and I never felt the pressure to drink when at the parties. I just didn't and that is it. Would you believe me if I told you I've never been drunk? I have never been drunk!

Drugs take the lives and careers of some of the greatest people. For example, just look at the life of Len Bias, a great athlete coming out of the University of Maryland. He was drafted by the Boston Celtics and signed a multimillion dollar contract. He was expected to become one of the greatest players of all time.

The very night he was drafted he made a choice that killed him. He never earned a penny of his contract. Drugs killed him. What a sad story.

How about Rush Limbaugh with painkillers? They got the best of him, and he ended up dealing with the embarrassment of checking into rehab. I am proud of him for handling the situation correctly. I am glad that he sought help before it was too late.

How about Chris Farley? Man, he was one of the best actors in the world. Remember on "Saturday Night Live" how he did that skit about Matt Foley, the motivational speaker? I loved that and loved him. It is sad to see with all that talent, he was still not satisfied with himself. He sought the artificial high because personally he was missing something within himself. He needed the women, the fame, the money, the alcohol, and the drugs. Now he is dead.

ALCOHOL IS A DRUG

Many of our youths today don't think that alcohol is a drug. It is. It impairs your thinking, your reflexes, and your ability to make rational choices. Alcohol abuse can lead to medical problems, unplanned pregnancies, suicide attempts, crimes such as assault and rape, and AIDS. Consider the following facts that were recently reported by SADD (Students against Destructive Decisions):

- One in three college students now drinks primarily to get drunk.
- 95 percent of violent crimes on campus are alcohol-related.
- 90 percent of all reported campus rapes occur when alcohol is being used by either the assailant or the victim or both.
- 60 percent of college women who have acquired sexually transmitted diseases, including AIDS and genital herpes, were under the influence of alcohol at the time they had intercourse.

Perhaps those stats don't do anything for you. Well then here are some that might make you think again.

- A 19-year-old Lewis University student fatally shot himself with a .38-caliber revolver in a game of Russian roulette. According to his roommate, the student apparently spun the chamber and pulled the trigger several times before the round fired, killing him instantly. Both students had been drinking prior to the incident.
- An 18-year-old University of Colorado freshman was killed after being thrown from the roof of a vehicle. The 18-year-old driver who had been drinking, as had all four passengers, tried to take a curve too fast and went off the side of the road, rolling the vehicle on its top.
- A Southwest Missouri State University freshman died after jumping off a seventh-story balcony during spring break on South Padre Island. Police said the student was tampering with a fire hose when security caught him. The student ran down the corridor and threw himself over the balcony. An autopsy showed that the 18-year-old had been drinking.

You are a smart person. You made the choice to read this book. I didn't want to spend a lot of time talking about this, but I thought it was necessary. Hey, just make the right choice. If you need further help, please visit my website, as I have a whole section on whom to call for the help you need.

It is when we TAKE TIME TO THINK about our choices before we act upon them that our inner self will direct us to RIGHTEOUSNESS.

Sometimes it is hard because it will require patience and going against what makes us happy. However, it is the TAKE-TIME-TO-THINK mantra that will always help us do the right thing.

Remember: *Do the difficult right over the easy wrong.*

What The Students Are Asking:

 How do you handle stress when one problem after another just lands on your shoulders?

- *Catherine C., Upper Perkiomen High School, PA*

Answer: I understand that some people just attract problems, but for the most part, problems occur because we bring them on ourselves. I literally, TAKE TIME TO THINK and do, "THE RIGHT THING!" This way I don't have to deal with problems one after another.

Recently, my daughter Tori and I were talking and she asked me a question. I responded, "Tori, just do what is right!" She responded in a 21 year old tone, "DAD, WHY IS IT THAT EVERY TIME I ASK YOU A QUESTION YOU ALWAYS SAY, "DO THE RIGHT THING?" My response to my daughter was very simple. I said, "Because when you do what is right you don't ever have to worry about problems or issues. Doing what is right just makes life so much easier."

So, to avoid stress is to do what is right, but when you are stressed you have to exercise the 4C's in life – Be Calm, Be Cool, Collect Yourself, and Stay in Control of your Emotions. Stress can beat you up pretty bad if you let it.

Lastly, learn how to breathe and relax yourself. Breathe in through your nose and exhale slowly out your mouth. Do this for about 3-5 minutes. It relaxes you.

Very lastly, journaling is a great way to relax and free yourself from stress. Journaling helps you to slow down your brain and your thought process. Get a journal and put the pen to the paper and write.

 With depression and suicide in teens becoming more and more common, what is the best way someone can help a depressed child?

- Parent, Facebook Message

Answer: First and foremost, get the child help. Seek professional counseling or therapy to learn how to deal with depression. Depression is serious and can be managed with the right professional counseling and medication. My personal and professional opinion is that depression is serious and shouldn't be taken care of outside of the professional help of a qualified professional.

CHAPTER SIX

WRITE DOWN YOUR GOALS

Goals are very important. He shoots! He scores! Important stuff. But there's even more to goals in life. Goals have a beginning and an end. You set them, go after them, and do everything in your power to attain them in the time you set for yourself.

Goals focus your attention. You will not be able to stay focused or measure your progress unless you clearly define your goals. When you have a clear understanding of your goals and can visualize what you want, then you will have the desire to work hard to reach them. The desire will ignite the spark inside you that pushes you toward the success. Once you feel the desire, your determination to succeed becomes more powerful than any feeling of giving up.

Not having a goal is like trying to drive a car without a road map to a place you have never visited. How can you expect to reach your destination without proper direction? The same is true of anything you wish to accomplish in life. You need a plan – a road map that leads you from point A to B.

So here is the time for you to write down some of your goals. The following SMART formula will help you. Write on a piece of paper the following:

GOALS I WANT TO ACCOMPLISH

List the goals you WILL accomplish daily, weekly, monthly, and annually. Have goals for one year, three years, five years and even beyond. Write down any and all of your dreams. Some you will reach, some you will not, and some will change. The important thing is to write them down.

Do that every year, reviewing last year's goals and adding new ones. Rewrite your goals. See them, read them, know them, list them, and change them whenever you want. The important thing is to write them down.

Write down as many as you desire. Don't be shy. This is your chance to dream big. Write down places you would like to visit, people you would like to meet, activities you would like to do, and things you would like to achieve. Write down whatever you desire in your heart.

After making your list, write beside each goal the exact date you WILL accomplish your goal. That is an important part of goal setting because it places a deadline on your goal. You have now obligated yourself to achieve it by a certain date because you are creating a contract with yourself. Take it another step further, and tell someone about it asking them to help hold you to it making it even harder for you to give up.

The contract with yourself stores the goals in your mind, just as you would store data in a computer. Now your list of goals becomes your checklist. It's the same as if you had listed items on a grocery checklist. A grocery checklist allows you to see and remember what you need to get at the store. A goal checklist allows you to see and remember what you desire to achieve in life.

Once your mind is programmed with the data of what you WILL accomplish, you begin moving toward achieving your goals. Before you realize it, you start to achieve your goals. Your dreams start to become realities!

It's like magic when you write down your goals and place a deadline on achieving them. Somehow, you begin to achieve them.

At the end of your goal checklist, after you have written down ALL of your goals, it is very important for you to sign and date the paper. That commits you to pursuing them because it is now a formal contract with yourself. Now you have no one to blame but yourself if you fail to pursue your goals.

Look at your goals every day when you wake up and/or before you go to bed. Keep showing and telling your mind that these are the things you WILL accomplish in your life.

SMART GOALS

SMART stands for: Specific, Measurable, Attainable, Realistic, and Timely.

SPECIFIC –

Be specific as to exactly what you want. You can't be too specific. Write it all down. Go for it.

Do you want a car? What kind of car? What color? Two doors or four doors? Hatchback, wagon, sedan, SUV, sports car or convertible?

Do you want a house? Ranch, split level, four bedrooms, three bedrooms, two baths or three baths? Two-car garage or three-car garage? Heated garage? Do you want an office, play room, furnished basement for the big screen television so you can watch your sports or just go down for the surround sound and chill while watching a nice movie?

MEASURABLE –

Lay your goals out as to when you want to attain them. How long will it take you? By when do you want to achieve the goal(s)? Have goals that are daily, weekly, monthly, and annually. Here is an example:

Daily –	1 Year –
Weekly –	3 Years –
Monthly –	5 Years –
3 Months –	10 Years –
6 Months –	

ATTAINABLE –

Can you do it in the time you have allotted yourself? Are you comfortable with the tasks you've outlined or are you trying to do too much too quickly? Have you set aside time just to chill? Is it really attainable?

REALISTIC –

Make your goals as realistic as you can. You can say, "Jeff, when I grow up I want to play in the NBA." But if you are 27 years old, 5'2" in the 9th grade, have one leg shorter than the other, and are blind in one eye, then that goal probably is not realistic. Spend time defining goals you desire and expect to achieve. Setting realistic goals doesn't mean thinking small. It's not a convenient way of limiting your dreams. If you start writing your goals with a poor attitude, it's easy to say any dream is unrealistic. Don't go there. It's a trap.

TIMELY –

Are you giving yourself enough time to reach the goals you are setting? Are you shortening the time line too much? You probably can't graduate college in two years. I mean you can, but should you reevaluate the time you are giving yourself?

YOUR PURPOSE

Your purpose in life is now your goal. Your purpose is what you do every day to reach and achieve the great success you are after. By staying in purpose you turn your desires into actions every day.

Without a purpose you have nothing driving you to reach the goals. Your purpose is never-ending. It is the track that keeps the train on course. It is the breakfast that holds you over to your next meal. It is the thread that connects the day from morning to afternoon to night.

When your friends want to go to the party and drink, but you are thinking that you have something else more productive to do, something that you haven't completed yet, that's when you are thinking of your purpose.

Your purpose keeps you on track and gives you the motivation to accomplish the day's work when the going gets tough. Your purpose gives you direction to reach your goals in the shortest amount of time.

What The Students Are Asking:

 Which is more important, focusing on short-term goals that can be achieved in the near future or long-term goals that may take a long span of time to achieve?
- *Brandon S., Rockwood Area High School, PA*

Answer: I don't think either is more important. Short-term goals are different than long-term goals. Short-term goals if written correctly and followed through with will lead you to the success of your long-term goals. Accomplishing the daily and weekly goals every week will lead you to success and accomplishing the long- term goals you set for one year, two year, five years down the road.

Here is an example: Let's say your goal is to get accepted to Carnegie Mellon. This is a long-term goal you might set in the 9th grade. The short-term goals are each quarterly marking period. You make short-term goals each marking period to be the best you can be and get the best grades possible.

As you can see, both long-term and short-term are equally important, but the short-term goals are more commonly focused on than the long-term goals are in the particular set of goals.

CHAPTER
SEVEN

PLAN FOR THE FUTURE – NOW

Most of your life will be affected by the career you choose. If you decide to become a shoemaker, be prepared at dinner parties to hear questions like "Can you make a size 29 look like a size six?" Do you have any idea what you want to do when you're out of school? If not, you're not alone. I would bet that 90 percent of the teenagers in America have no clue. I would also bet that the majority of the 90 percent who don't have a clue don't even think about it. I never did.

You need to start getting a clue, NOW! You're not expected to know what will be your career for the rest of your life. But you do need to begin researching certain careers. Why? Your life will revolve around your career. You will most likely work five days and forty hours a week, 235 days, and 2,040 hours a year, and about 7,000 days and 80,000 hours of your life. I bet you never thought of it like that. Now think of this: doing something you hate. Not something to look forward to, is it?

How many times have you heard someone say, "I hate my job?" You don't want to be in a situation where you hate going to work every day.

Trust in the Advice of Elders

If you've heard me speak before you know I speak a lot about my wife's grandfather. I love that story that I share. You can listen and watch it on my website or on YouTube.

Well, in that story I always open it talking to teens about expectations and objectives. I ask about disappointments we've had in our lives. We've all had disappointment, right? Sure we have and we will continue to have disappointment when we continue to have expectations, but here is a way to rid yourself of some of life's challenges and obstacles. Find people in your life that you trust and respect. People whose opinions you value and go to them.

It's that simple. Think about it for a second. You ask an 80 year old person – man or woman a question and you'll get a two minute answer filled with over 60 years of experiences, books they've read, people they've met, jobs they've had, successes and failures that they've encountered too.

Isn't that awesome experience in life? To have people that you can ask a question and they can give you real life answers. It's like human Google, but without the screen and keyboard, plus you learn social skills this way too. HA! I thought that was funny!

CHOOSING A CAREER

In the episode of MTV's "MADE" that I was in, I worked with 18-year-old Alyssa of Moundsview, Minn., a high school senior who had dozens of interests, but no idea of what sort of career she should pursue. First, we got her to narrow the list down to twenty. From that, we narrowed it down to five, then to three: massage therapy, urban landscaping and café operator. We put her in work situations so she spent at least three days in each occupation. After all that, she decided performing arts and theater was really where she wanted to be. So we took her to Chicago to audition for a comedy sports theater. She performed live and nailed it. They even offered her a scholarship. So after all those twists and turns, she found her passion. You can, too.

Start by finding something meaningful, rewarding, and fulfilling. If you identify the things that make you happy, you will begin to get a clearer idea of what you may want to do when you get out of school. It may be acting or sports, mathematics or music, speaking or science. The key is to identify the activities which make you feel good about what you've accomplished.

Ask yourself the following two questions. They will help you to decide which career will make you happy:

1. Which career really excites and energizes me?
2. Which career would make me feel most fulfilled?

Once you have identified a career that you think will fulfill you, give you meaning, and be rewarding, then make a commitment to yourself to pursue your ambition. Gather as much information as you can. If you can find people who work in that field, talk to them and find out what they like or don't like about their job. Don't listen to those who try to discourage you. Many people dream of working a certain job or in a particular industry. But few accomplish their dreams if they listen when others tell them that it's not possible.

You have the ability to pursue and land any career you desire. Don't listen to those who try to discourage you. Those are probably the very people who have never, and will never, have the career they desire for themselves. Just because they haven't done it, they think that you can't. They're wrong, and tell them I said so!

Start laying the foundation now. "So, how do I lay the foundation?" you ask. It is quite simple. First, as I mentioned above, you should find out everything you can about the career you have chosen using every resource you have available. Secondly, you need to begin interning in the Real World. Work with your parents or teachers to arrange for you to go into various businesses to work for a day, week, month, or even the entire summer. You will get an inside look at what it is really like to work in that career. You can't get that experience in a classroom or from a textbook. You will see what you like and dislike. That is also called OJT – On the Job Training. You may even find a company that will have a job waiting for you when you graduate.

SUCCESS VERSUS SIGNIFICANCE

There is richness in material gain, or there is richness in people. Richness in material is the gain of "toys." The richness in people is the gain of relationships and friendship. Which do you prefer? I have experienced the people and the relationships; I have also experienced the acquiring of toys in my life. Which do I prefer? Having had both worlds, I will take the relationships and friendships any day over the toys.

How do you define success? How do you define significance? Success is what others see, whereas significance is a result of the difference you have made and the feeling you have gained from making a difference. If you have to tell of your success, then you haven't really been a success, and people aren't impressed. If someone else can tell of your success, then you gained the respect of others and have achieved significance.

NETWORKING OR QUILT-WORKING

College will teach you that whom you know plays a significant role in what you do or whom you become. However, please let me add this, as I have always thought more about quilt-working then networking:

Networking says, "Who is out there that has the resources I need, and how do I get in contact with them?" Quilt-working says that there are many different pieces, colors, fabrics, patterns, shapes, and sizes, and they all help to make the one piece we call a quilt. I have always lived my life believing that everyone is part of the puzzle. The more people I get to meet and know, the more I grow, the more people I can help, and the more people who can help me.

Networking says, "Who can help me?" while quilt-working takes it a step further and says, "I need your help and I will help you and together we can reach our dreams." Everybody is part of the puzzle of life. It doesn't matter if you are black or white, Jewish or Protestant, Catholic or Hindu, Latino or Asian. It doesn't matter if you go home and light candles, burn incense, throw salt over your shoulder, or run around your house naked. The question is, "Who are you working with, who do you trust, who can you help, who can you believe in, and who believes in you?" Quilt-working begins where networking leaves off because quilt-working brings together individuals and makes them part of the puzzle.

The more people you know the further ahead you are. You meet people every day, but do you keep in contact with them?

Do you have an address book? Get one and use it. The most valuable tool you can have is an address book. Use it for Christmas cards and to keep in touch. Everybody you meet who touches your life in some way should be in your address book. Their full names, significant others' names, addresses, cities, states, zips, phone numbers, email addresses, dates of birth, etc. should be included in the address book. You can buy one for a $1.99 at any Staples, Office Max, or Hallmark store.

"You never know how far a contact can take you. Stay in touch with everyone."

– JEFF YALDEN

I think communication is the most important skill for anyone to become successful. You communicate every day with people in every part of your life. That includes school, sports, business and family situations, talking on the phone, emailing, instant messaging, and talking to groups. How well you communicate will determine people's perception of you, meaning how people think of you as a person.

Developing good communication skills as a teenager can make you very successful for the rest of your life. One of the key ingredients of successful communication skills is making contacts. The contacts you make every day will help you succeed.

In life, I can promise you that people will be your shortcuts to your success. The more people you know, the more opportunities you will have, and the richer your life will become.

Every person you build a relationship with for the rest of your life should be listed in your little address book. Whom you meet and what you talked about should all be listed in there, and you should make a habit of keeping in touch with them at least once a year.

Get to know as many people as you can. Soon you'll need a more expensive address book, but it will be the best investment you'll ever make in your life. Before the car, fancy computers, nice offices, or clothes, buy that nice address book and make it your everything. Use it every day.

You never know who is influential, or who knows whom. In today's world, whom you know can help you get ahead faster than anything else. Diversify your contacts by meeting different kinds of people (quilt-working). Take the initiative to introduce yourself, start a conversation, and build a rapport with people.

Equally as important as meeting people is staying in touch. Meeting a person once will not help you in the future. You need to build a relationship, get their address and phone number, list them in your address book, then stay in touch forever with that person even when their address and phone number changes. No excuses.

One thing I do now in my business is write a newsletter monthly. I do that to keep in touch and to let people know where I am and what I have been up to. It is a way to continue the relationship. Perhaps, they may need a speaker in the future, and someone has forwarded them my email address. Maybe they forgot about me. Perhaps they visited my website and forgot that I am a speaker, but on a monthly basis they receive my newsletter by email. It is just a way to say hello on a monthly basis and to let them know I care about them.

You can send thank-you notes, birthday cards, Christmas cards, Thanksgiving cards, anniversary cards, and just hello letters. Call them periodically and occasionally get together for a quick visit. Keep in touch.

Here is proof that it works ...

In 2003, I had the honor of speaking at the Florida State Student Council Association's conference. I met a great lady who has become a friend whom I respect and admire. Her name is Carrie Coons. She was the executive director of the Florida State Student Council and National Honor Society. There were a few times that I needed something and knew that she could lead me in the right direction.

Carrie and I were talking one day, and she gave me the name of someone who is directly responsible, the executive director of the Southern Association of Student Councils. Her name is Patti Ireland. Well, I wrote a little email and introduced myself to Patti and said I would be honored if she would pass my name along as a possible speaker for the association's next conference. As a result of Carrie and Patti knowing each other, I was selected to be one of the keynote speakers at the Southern Association of Student Councils conference in Humble, Texas. I had an awesome time, and it resulted in my booking about four state conferences as a result, which in turn led to meeting more people, sharing new experiences, and making my business grow.

Carrie is on my list to receive my newsletter and so is Patti Ireland. Just this past week, Carrie also sent an email to me about a lady in Michigan who is seeking a speaker for her advisors. I called right away and talked with her and gave Carrie's name as a point of contact about the success we had with her students.

Carrie, I love you. Let me know what I can do for you now.

Don't be afraid to introduce yourself to people, and stay in touch with everyone you meet. That includes all teenage friends, high school friends, college friends, teachers, professors, sports teammates, business associates, your parents' friends, your relatives' friends, people you work with, people you work for – EVERYONE! You just never know where it could lead.

CHAPTER EIGHT

SUCCESS AND MONEY –
THE BOTTOM LINE

*"We have screwed up our youth today.
We as a society have taught them that the only
way you can become successful is if you make
a lot of money."*

– UNKNOWN

You need to understand a few things about success and money. They're really, really nice. But there's more to life. First, having money does not mean you are successful. Drug dealers have a lot of money, big homes, and drive some nice fancy cars. Does that mean they are successful? No! Success is much more than money.

One of the best definitions of success I have ever heard came from Legendary UCLA basketball coach John Wooden. Coach Wooden's definition of success is:

"Peace of mind is a direct result of self-satisfaction in knowing you did your best to become the best that you are capable of becoming."

– JOHN WOODEN

Success is all about feeling good about yourself as a result of what you do because you know that deep down inside, you did your best and contributed to this wonderful world we live in. You made a difference. Success is about happiness – happiness within yourself and the life you lead.

There is nothing wrong with wanting to have money. The problem exists when you make money your main focus. You become greedy; your life becomes twisted, and you become very selfish. If you work hard and do what makes you happy, then the money will follow.

Think about finding a career that is rewarding, meaningful, and ful-filling. Now think of doing that job and making average money. Compare that feeling to working a career you despise. You dread Monday mornings, the drive makes you sick, the people make your skin crawl, but yeah you are making great money. The weekend comes, and what are you like? The difference between the two is that you can live happi-ly with the money you make but all the money in the world can't make you happy. Work for the enjoyment of the job, not the money. Remember it's in the workplace where you'll spend most of your time. Why not make it a place that you enjoy?

Have you ever heard, "Money doesn't grow on trees?" Whoever said it was right. Because it doesn't grow on trees and doesn't come to us as often as we'd like, don't you think we should save what we have? Most teenagers and adults think that spending is a hobby and that you can always squeeze an extra $20 out of your pocket or someone else's. I have news for you: other people will not always be there to play Mr. or Ms. Bank Teller. There will come a time in the very near future when you will be responsible for earning and managing your own money. You will soon find out that spending is not as much fun when it's your own money. It's time to learn some basic principles of good money management.

SAVING MONEY

Saving money means that you don't spend it. That is right: no spending! By that I mean no more $120 sneakers, no more $100 BLING, no more $65 Aber-Crappy and Fitch, and no more $50 Tommy Pull-My-Finger. Don't let your peers spend your money! The idea of saving is to keep more than you spend. The more you can save now, the more you will have later. Remember this, it's not how much you earn; it's how much you keep.

The problem is, most teenagers don't have much self-control when it comes to saving money. Listed below are a few tips that will help you save at least a portion of what you have.

1. Put a portion of any money you earn in a savings account at a bank. Ask your parents or an adult to help you open your own account.
2. Be a smart shopper. Do not buy things just for the fun of it. Buy only what is necessary (Buying $120 basketball sneakers when you can find some for $39.99 is not necessary.)
3. Leave your money at home when you go to the mall or other stores. You are more likely to spend money when in the mall or stores. You can always go home to get money if there is something you absolutely must buy.
4. Follow the "Golden Rule" to becoming wealthy. Take 10 percent of anything you earn and put it away forever. That means you never touch it unless it's an extreme emergency (buying a new

game for your Xbox is not an emergency). If you continue to put 10 percent away from every paycheck for the next 20-30 years, you will become very wealthy.

(I highly suggest the book **"The Wealthy Barber"** for all teenagers and young adults.)

CREDIT CARDS

I remember when I received my first credit card. I immediately ran to Kmart and bought stuff for my office. I had no computer, but I had a desk, and now I had files, paper, a stapler, a hole puncher, pens, pencils, books, calendars, etc. Pretty soon the credit cards kept coming, and so did the nice computer. It was awesome. I had a nice office; little did I know that I had to pay it all back. To make matters worse, I was charged interest. That meant I would repay more than the money I spent. Ouch!

Also, when you get a credit card at 9 percent interest, please read the details and fine print. Just send in one payment late and that 9 percent increases to about 19-24 percent without them even telling you ahead of time, and, YES, they can do that.

Charging items on a credit card is like taking a loan from a bank. It must be repaid, with interest. It's not free money and could get you in serious financial trouble if you go on a spending spree. Listed below are a few tips to help you avoid financial destruction:

1. Only charge what you know you can pay off when the monthly bill arrives. Never charge your card to the maximum limit. The higher your balance, the less money from your payment goes to paying off what you "borrowed." Most of it will go toward paying off the interest on your loan.

2. Keep the receipts from all purchases so you can keep track of how much you have been charged.
3. If you can't pay cash for it, you probably don't need it.

Remember, credit is not free money. It is money you must repay, plus interest. The best way to use a credit card is to not use it but store it for emergency situations.

INVESTING

That simply means to put money into stocks, companies, 401Ks, IRAs, businesses, etc. in order to get a profit. When you invest, you are putting your money into something that you believe will grow your original investment and make you money. If it grows, you will receive more money back than you originally put into it. That is what investing is all about.

One of the most common ways to invest is to purchase stocks of companies. The way to buy stocks is through a stockbroker. Buying a few shares of stocks at a young age is one of the best ways to get started learning about investing and the stock market. A good way to begin investing is to buy stocks of companies whose products or services you already use. The following are a few examples:

Mc Donalds	Microsoft	Reebook
Burger King	Dell	nike
Coca-Cola	Apple	IBM
PepsiCo	Disney	Sony

Ask yourself which products or services you and your friends use, then find out information on those companies. It may be worth buying a few shares if there is demand for their products or services. If you can't afford to buy the stocks, practice investing without spending any money. Pick some stocks, write down the number of shares and the prices you would have paid. Then follow their progress over weeks and months to see how well you've done. You'll learn many valuable lessons and the best thing is all you have to spend is your time.

Another investment vehicle is stock mutual funds. A stock mutual fund is like an Easter egg basket filled with eggs. The basket is the mutual fund and the eggs are the individual stocks. When you buy a mutual fund, you own a piece of the stocks in your basket. How well the stocks do in the fund determines how well the overall fund performs. Mutual funds are a good way to diversify your risk because you own pieces of many stocks rather than just buying one stock. Some mutual fund companies will allow you to start investing with as little as $50- $100.

HOW TO BECOME A MILLIONAIRE

Forget about "Get-Rich-Quick" schemes. The best way to create wealth is by investing for the long term. The key is to start early.

If you are working as a teenager, great! If you are not, then you may want to consider getting a job so you can earn a little money to invest. Think about it. If you are like most teenagers, you probably live at home with your parents and have no bills or financial obligations. If you were to get a part-time job, you could earn enough to invest and begin creating your fortune. Consider the following example:

Suppose you were to get a part-time job and worked only 15 hours per week and got paid $5 per hour. You would earn $75 per week. That's $300 per month and $3,600 per year. Let's suppose that $600 of the $3,600 you earn a year is what you owe to Uncle Sam for income tax. That would leave you with $3,000.

Since you are working and have earned income, you can invest up to $2,000 a year in an Individual Retirement Account (IRA). An IRA is an account that allows you to put money into it to be used for your retirement. You do not pay any taxes on the growth of the money until it is withdrawn, usually between the ages of 60-65.

If you invest $2,000 a year from age 15 to 19 and never invest any more after age 19, (assuming your annual return of at least 12 percent) your money would be worth more than $1,000,000 by age 591/2. Dude, that is AWESOME!

Compounding interest creates a huge snowball effect. Your interest keeps accumulating over the years without losing a portion of your growth to income taxes.

If you withdraw any portion of your money before age 591/2, there is a 10 percent penalty on any money taken out and it is also subject to income tax.

If you take $2,000 of the $3,000 you earn from your part-time job and invest it in an IRA, and you do that from age 15 to 19 (five years), you will become a millionaire. The following table illustrates how your money would grow.

Age	Year	Investment	15%	14%
15	1	$2,000	$2,300	$2,280
16	2	$2,000	$4,945	$4,879
17	3	$2,000	$7,987	$7,842
18	4	$2,000	$11,485	$11,220
19	5	$2,000	$15,507	$15,071
20	6	0	$17,834	$17,181
30	16	0	$72,147	$63,694
40	26	0	$291,874	$236,127
50	36	0	$1,180,794	$875,374
59	45	0	$4,153,888	$2,846,668

Age	Year	Investment	13%	12%
15	1	$2,000	$2,260	$2,240
16	2	$2,000	$4,814	$4,749
17	3	$2,000	$7,700	$7,559
18	4	$2,000	$10,961	$10,706
19	5	$2,000	$14,645	$14,230
20	6	0	$16,549	$15,938
30	16	0	$56,176	$49,501
40	26	0	$190,696	$153,743
50	36	0	$647,328	$477,502
59	45	0	$1,944,602	$1,324,150

(The author is only offering ideas and suggestions for investing. He is not promising or guaranteeing any investment returns or performance and is not liable for any losses that may occur to your investments. Consult your parents or a licensed financial advisor before starting any investing.)

The bottom line is to start saving at an early age and find someone you trust and whose opinions you value. Start with buying a little stock or investing in an IRA. Put away the money now at an early age, and then you are set for life.

The chart on page 86 will show you how the money makes money from itself. The money keeps on compounding (making more money) even after you stop investing. The money will continue to grow. It may not grow on trees, but it will grow just the same.

What The Students Are Asking:

 What is true happiness, and is it possible to achieve that "true happiness?"
- Max S., *Radnor High School*, PA

Answer: True happiness is different for each and every person you will ask. For me, I think true happiness comes down to two things:

- When you lay your head on your pillow at night there is three questions you should ask yourself:
    - Is my life rewarding
    - Is my life fulfilling
    - Is my life meaningful

- The second is on Sunday are you dreading the Monday work-week?

I measure my happiness on knowing my life is rewarding, fulfilling, and meaningful. I also measure my life in knowing that whether it be Friday night or Monday morning, I love work, I love my family, and I love life.

So, in short, is it possible to achieve true happiness? For me, absolutely! What about for you? Absolutely! Just don't complicate what happiness really is.

 If there was one message or story you were able to say to everyone what would it be?
- *Hedy Z., Joaquin Miller Middle School, CA*

Answer: The message I would want to share with everyone would be the unconditional love we receive from dogs. I've never experienced unconditional love like I have from having a dog that for 12 years touched my heart.

Again, if you've heard me speak most recently, you know that I lost my best friend, Chase. Chase was a chocolate lab that for 12 years was my best friend. I'll never forget that day when he was 6 weeks old and my wife and I were able to take him home. My life changed so much as a result of having a dog to love, but also a dog that loved me more than what humans can understand what love is.

Everywhere I would go, Chase would go too. Any door I would enter at any time of day or night, Chase would greet me. Anybody that would come to the house, it didn't matter who they were, it didn't matter what color they were or what they wore...Chase loved and accepted every one. Chase didn't judge. Chase didn't choose. Chase just automatically accepted and loved unconditionally.

On May 3, 2012 my wife called me at 6:30 am and told me that Chase had died in his sleep. I drove home so fast and when I walked in the house, I asked my wife where he was, and she told me he was asleep under my desk in my office. I went into my office and I sat down and I cried like a baby. I miss Chase more than you could imagine.

As I sat there I realized that for 12 years I took him for granted. The 12 years that he graced my heart with his presence I sat there thinking not one last time did I say, "Thank you!" Not one last time did I say, "I love you!"

My heart is still broken and I'm not ready for another dog, but the lesson I learned is that love should be unconditional. Why can't we accept and love others the way dogs can love their masters and their friends?

Can't we just live our lives the way dogs live theirs?
I miss you buddy!

CHAPTER NINE

NEVER STOP LEARNING

"Education is the only thing you have left after you have forgotten everything you have learned."

– UNKNOWN

You have likely heard the phrase Knowledge is Power! How true it is. They should make an X-Man. Call him Know-Pow. One punch, and pow, you know better. Let's face it: The more you learn, the more you grow. The more you grow, the more diverse your background becomes. The more diverse your background becomes, the more valuable you will be. Therefore, you will have more opportunities.

The problem with most people is, they think they know it all. People who know it all are stopping themselves from learning. When you think you know it all, your mind isn't open to new ideas and opinions. They stagnate. They tell the same lame stories, and they'll have the same skills 20 years from now as they do today.

When you open your mind to new ideas and opinions, you become more interesting. Make it a point to learn something new every day, whether in or out of school.

It's not only important to pay attention in school, but also outside of school. Pay attention to current events that are happening in everyday life. Take the initiative to keep learning.

Did you know that if you stay on top of current events every day you can hold yourself in an enjoyable conversation with anyone? You are bound to find something in common if you just keep learning. You'll be surprised at how much you know. Knowledge is not only power but it gives you self-confidence and allows you to meet and talk to more people than you could ever imagine.

How do you keep learning, though? It is very easy. Communicate and listen, write, read, and watch TV. Listen to talk shows on the radio instead of listening to music. Let's take some time and start with communicating and listening since they go hand in hand.

COMMUNICATE AND LISTEN

"We have two ears and one mouth.
We should listen more than we talk."

– UNKNOWN

Every day of your life, you find yourself communicating. Every time you communicate with someone, you have the opportunity to learn something new if you just take the time to listen. Most people communicate and never listen. They want to talk and get their own opinions out rather than listen to the opinions of others. Talk to a variety of people – people of different ages, nationalities, and backgrounds. Don't be intimidated because they may be a little different from you.

It's easy to get people talking. Simply ask them questions. Go back to the section when I talked about "Listening to your elders . . ."

People love talking about themselves, especially if they feel they are teaching you how to do something. It makes them feel important. Questions can always start a conversation and comprise the key to keeping it going. Never be afraid to ask people questions because you believe they'll think less of you. Asking questions is how they learned, and it's how you'll learn and gain knowledge.

WRITING

Another great way to learn is by writing. That includes letters, research papers, and even a book! One of my favorite exercises that I have teenagers do in my seminars is called the "Learn about Myself" exercise. Try it; you'll be amazed at what you will learn about yourself.

Write the following on a piece of paper, and then answer them honestly.

1. Which five things do I most value in my life?
2. Which five goals are most important to me?
3. Who are the five most important people in my life?
4. What would I do if I won $1,000,000 today?
5. What would I do if I only had six months to live?
6. What one thing would I try if I knew I could not fail?
7. What one thing would I change about the world?

After the completion of the questions, I then ask this:

If, for twenty-four hours, seven days a week, I see you, but you can't see me, what would I see you doing that shows you place a value on any of your answers listed above?

You don't need to show your answers to anyone. The exercise is to help you learn about yourself. Do that exercise at least once a year. Your answers will probably change every year as you mature.

Here is another exercise that I love. Take a few pieces of paper or a journal and write at the top: "Who am I?" and "What do I want?" Now, for thirty minutes write nonstop your answers to those two questions.

At the end of the thirty minutes, reread what you wrote and take out any negative answers. Get another piece of paper. On that sheet of paper, turn the negative answers into positives and rework the questions from Why to How. An example is as follows:

If you wrote, "I am negative and too selfish," turn the question from "Why am I like that?" to "How can I make that a positive characteristic trait about myself?"

For example, "How can I become more positive and unselfish?" Now you have asked a better question and it is up to you to take personal responsibility to make the change.

The difference here is that "why" questions leave you blaming the circumstances around you and not taking personal responsibility. "How" questions get you to take personal responsibility and to come up with the answers and take action.

VALUE CARD

Here is the quickest way to raise your self-esteem. Get an index card. On the top of it write "Value Card." List five things on it that you value. It could be family, faith, friends, education, money, cars, etc. What do you value? There is no right or wrong. They are your values, and nobody can take that away from you. Your values will change as you mature. Here is my personal value card.

My Value Card:
1. Faith (My relationship with my Higher Power)
2. Family and friends (It's fine to put them together)
3. Education (Always be learning)
4. Fitness and health
5. Time

Now you can take that a step further. After every value, write a paragraph on WHY you value that. Here is an example of mine:

My Value Card:
- Faith (My relationship with my Higher Power)
  - I thank my Higher Power for the ability to do what I do and for the love I have in my life. Without His support, energy, enthusiasm, and love, I wouldn't be who I am today. He uses me to reach my audience. He works through me to speak to you.

- Family and friends (It's fine to put them together)
  - Family provided me with support, food, clothing, and the wisdom to start my life. Friends are there for encouragement, support, listening, and communicating. I get love from both family and friends, and that is very important in self-esteem.

- Education (Always be learning)
    - Education is the only thing I have left after I have forgotten everything I have learned. Seek every day to be smarter and more knowledgeable than I was the day before.

- Fitness and health
    - If I am not in shape, I am not In-Purpose. Eat right for energy. Eat to live; don't live to eat.

- Time
    - My time is limited so I appreciate every moment I have. Time is sensitive, fragile, and limited. Take advantage of the little time I have to maximize everything I can out of it.

READING

The first thing I would suggest is to read the newspaper every day to stay informed about current events. Remember, by you staying on top of current events, you can hold your own in any conversation, intellectual or otherwise, with anyone.

You never know when you are going to be put into a position where you will need to discuss a current event. If you only focus on reading one part of the paper, it could make you feel uncomfortable in certain situations. So read the sports section and the headlines, your local news, and world events.

Read books on self-help; read articles in magazines. It's been proven that you can increase your knowledge and even your vocabulary simply by reading. Keep a dictionary nearby when you read. If you don't understand a word, don't just breeze by it. Take a minute to look it up and understand the definition. You will be learning a new word. Also, when speaking with someone who uses a word you are not familiar with, don't be afraid to ask what that word means. That someone will be impressed because you asked, and you will also learn a new word.

WATCHING TV

Have your parents ever complained to you that you watch too much television? They're not entirely wrong. Television is OK if you watch it in moderation and give yourself a time limit on what to watch. You don't want to waste your life by becoming a couch potato eating potato chips and drinking soda.

Television is great if you can learn from what you are watching. I'm not saying you shouldn't watch the nonsensical sitcoms. Hey, I love "The Biggest Loser," "Hardcore Pawn," "Cops," and sports.

What I am simply saying is that there are certain times when watching the television to learn is OK. Just as you read the newspaper to keep up on current events, you should also watch the local or world news. It takes only thirty minutes of local news to get updated on the most important stories.

Try not to watch anything negative before you go to bed. What goes in as you close your eyes at night also wakes up with you. So watch something positive and happy so that you wake up positive and happy.

In addition to the news, there are other quality programs that can serve as informative and educational outlets, such as PBS and the Discovery Channel. I also think ESPN is informative to keep updated in the world of sports.

I am not telling you to avoid watching movies, either. I am a big fan of some great movies. There are some great movies out there that everyone can learn from. Here are two that can teach you some important success principles:

"Rocky" (I and II)

Remember when Sylvester Stallone played boxer Rocky Balboa and he had the chance to fight Apollo Creed for the world heavyweight boxing title? No one gave him a chance. But no matter how bad Rocky was beaten up or how many times he was knocked down in the fight, he kept getting up. In "Rocky II," he became the heavyweight champion and proved that you can accomplish your dreams if you simply "go for it" and keep getting up when you're knocked down.

"Rudy"

This is a story of a student who didn't have the grades to get into his dream school, the University of Notre Dame. After going to another school and improving his grades, his dream came true. The University of Notre Dame accepted him. Then he tried out for the football team. His dream was to play one play in a real game, but he was much smaller than the other players and not as athletic. He never lost focus of his dream. Finally, he got the chance to play, sacked the quarterback, and at the end of the game, he was carried off the field on the shoulders of his teammates. No other player since Rudy has ever been carried off the field at the University of Notre Dame. It's a great movie about pursuing your dreams and not quitting.

CHAPTER
TEN

IF NOT YOU – WHO?

You have to believe in yourself regardless of any circumstances, anything that happened in the past, family backgrounds, adversities, etc. The belief in yourself is the most important habit you can learn to adopt. As you journey through life you will meet people who tell you that you're not smart enough to succeed. You will meet people who tell you that you don't have the ability to succeed. And you will certainly meet people who just don't believe in you or your abilities. So if you don't believe in yourself and the dreams you desire, then who will? Your big sister? Phsssh.

CONDITION YOUR MIND

You can't achieve anything unless you first believe it. Condition your mind to believe that you WILL achieve your dreams.

Your brain is a muscle. Like any other muscle in your body, it needs to be exercised in order for it to grow, become stronger, and increase its performance. The way to accomplish that is through proper exercise of your muscle (brain). Like any other muscle, stop using it, and you lose it.

Bill Gates is the richest man in America, with an estimated net worth of about $60 billion. (That's right, billion!) He is the founder and president of Microsoft. You have undoubtedly used computer software designed by his company.

In a recent interview, Bill was asked how he is able to develop unique ideas and concepts that continuously put Microsoft ahead of all other computer software companies. His answer was amazing, yet very simple.

Bill told a story of his childhood. He said that one day his mother could not find him anywhere in the house. Finally, she opened the closet door and found him sitting there in the dark closet. When his mother asked him why he was sitting in a dark closet, he replied, "I'm thinking."

Bill went on in the interview to stress how important it is to exercise your brain because it responds to repetitive exercise.

I like the quote that says, "Repetition is the mother of skill," meaning that in order for you to improve or increase performance, you need to practice the fundamentals over and over again.

Studies have indicated that it takes approximately 21-30 days to create a new habit. That means that if you want to change or create a belief in your mind, it should become a natural habit after working on it for 21-30 days.

"We are what we repeatedly do.
Excellence then, is not an act, but a habit."

– ARISTOTLE

RIGHTS AND PRIVILEGES VERSUS
RESPONSIBILITIES AND OBLIGATIONS

It was April of 2003. I was speaking at a youth conference in Utah when a bunch of state police officers surrounded me after my program. My first response was, "Oh no! I'm caught; they got me." Then I realized I didn't do anything. They asked me a question that I will never forget. They asked me what I thought was the difference between today's youth and the youth of 20 years ago. I thought long and hard and replied, "I think today's young people are thinking about their rights and privileges when twenty years ago they were thinking about their responsibilities and obligations."

What I am trying to say is simply this: you want and think you deserve rights and certain privileges, and I agree. However, rights and privileges are earned as a result of your earning TRUST. When people trust you, they tend to give you more rights and privileges. Therefore, you need to understand that once you fulfill your responsibilities and obligations, then your rights and privileges will be greater. Does that make sense? Do what you're supposed to do, when you should be doing it, at the time you should be doing it, and people will trust you; therefore, you will gain greater rights and privileges. Don't ever overlook the simple concept that it's the responsibilities and obligations that give you the opportunity to earn more rights and privileges.

I decided at a young age that my intelligence and ability were not going to get me the great success and significance I wanted, nor that I thought I deserved. Therefore, I chose to dedicate my life to hard work, making good choices and having a good atittude through tough times. I knew there were people who were a lot smarter than I. I knew there were people who were better athletically, more gifted academically, and more suited intellectually. However, I wasn't going to let someone out-work me. I was committed to being more prepared and hungry than the next person in going after what I wanted to achieve, what I thought I deserved.

Today, I live a great life as a simple result of my commitment to work hard, my attitude, and carefully making good choices – TAKE TIME TO THINK. I take great pride in my work ethic and credit my family's ethic with rubbing off on me.

The thrill of achieving your goals and dreams is knowing that you put in the time and worked hard for it. Whether it is receiving an "A" in school, getting an academic or athletic scholarship, landing a great job, earning a million dollars, helping a charity, or whatever, the satisfaction of knowing that it was your dedication, your commitment, and your effort is what makes achieving a goal worthwhile.

Let me also say this: I didn't do well in school. I scored a 680 and a 610 on my SATs. I grew up with a learning disability, but now I realize that I just learn differently. I graduated 128th out of 133 students. I always thought I was stupid and didn't have the ability. I realize now that I didn't commit to being the best and working hard at an early age. My point is simply this: work hard and commit to being the best you can. Whether you get an "A," a "B," or maybe even a "C" doesn't matter. Just do the best you can. If you did the best you can and a "B" or "C" is the best you can do, then you should be proud.

Every night when you lay your head on the pillow, ask yourself this question: "Did I give today my very best?" Also ask, "Am I a better person today than I was yesterday as a result of my hard work?" That is what I am talking about. If you aren't committed to working hard then you aren't committed to succeeding in what you do.

Commit yourself to working harder than everyone you know. Don't let them out-work you. They might be more gifted, may have more money, nicer clothes, and a nicer car, but a work ethic and commitment to excellence come from within your heart and soul. I promise you that if you commit to working hard you'll achieve what you want and more.

Today, I spoke at Marion Center Jr. Sr. High School in Marion Center, PA. Also Penns Manor High School came to the program. It was an awesome day where they broadcasted my talk to the middle schools in the two communities as well. What a great honor. Well, the Principal of Marion Center Jr. Sr. High School was a gentleman by the name of Matthew Jioio. What an awesome guy he was and a great school he runs. I'll cherish what he said when we were talking.

"I'd hire someone with heart any day ove someone with talent!"

- MATT JIOIO

Prinicpal, Marion Center Jr. Sr. High School

I have a business where I teach other people what I've done with my life. Really! If someone wants to be a professional motivational speaker and they hire me as a consultant I have them come spend a full day at my office and I teach them everything I know about 20 years in this business.

I charge them $4500 for the day and I give them everything I know. Why so much money do I charge? For one, I want them to be serious and I will tell them that I will make you a millionaire but I will not do the work for you. They have to choose whether or not they see the value in what I have to offer. Secondly, I am saving them hundreds of thousands of dollars in mistakes I've made.

Why do I do this? Why am I willing to give away my secrets and lessons learned over the years? Aren't they competition? Sure they are, but the reality is I know that no matter what I am going to out work them, out market them, and I'll be willing to out speak them. I have more heart and I am more hungry. I am less greedy. I am more grateful.

You see, I am not worried about giving away secrets because the reality is most people want the work done for them. Few people are unwilling to do it themselves. I am not worried a bit!

Having said all this, remember that your responsibilities is you being true to yourself. Your obligations are the commitments you make. This hard work and desire give you the rights and privliges you deserve. Rights and privliges doesn't come before hard work, responsibilities, and obligations. Don't ever forget that. The world owes you nothing!

CHAPTER ELEVEN

BE GRATEFUL

I'm grateful every day! I'm grateful that I have an awesome wife that has tolerated me and my issues over the past 17 years. I'm grateful I have two beautiful and talented daughters. I'm grateful that my dog Chase taught me more about unconditional love than any other experience or person in my life. I'm grateful for the little things in my life: my house, my friends, my nieces and nephews, my life, my office, my employees, my walkway, my trees, my pond and my 26 fish and counting. I live with gratitude every day!

One of the best exercises I have ever done is the Grateful Journal I keep. Every day, I write down five things I am grateful for, and no day can be a repeat of the day before. Every single day is a new day and a day to come up with five new things to be grateful for. Try it. It's hard after a while. However, it really teaches you to appreciate the little things in life. Here's an example:

Grateful Journal (date)

1. My freedom
2. My friends
3. Financial success
4. Air travel
5. My family

Then you do another day. Remember, the new day has to have a completely new list. Nothing identical. So many things to be grateful for:

1. Parents asleep when you come home late.
2. Teacher forgetting to collect the homework assignment you forgot to do.
3. Drunk residents to whom you delivered a pizza (big tippers).
4. Your sister's Mariah Carey CD getting too scratched to play.
5. Finding toilet paper when you reach for it.

That little piece of work has taught me many things, including a simple appreciation for our everyday existence in a world that is second to none. I mean, every day, I stop and think about how grateful I am to travel and work with youths. I am grateful that I can get on a plane at 8:00 p.m. on the East Coast and be doing a 7:30 a.m. school assembly on the West Coast.

When was the last time you stopped to think about our ability to travel so easily? How about the opportunity to just see different cultures, meet new people, see different lifestyles, and frequent great parts of the country?

I have learned what's really important in life – faith, good health, family, and friends. We take all that for granted way too much. How about personal safety? I travel close to 250,000 miles a year. I go from flight to rental car to hotel. I wake up and speak and do it all over again. The fact that I have not had any major challenges, accidents, delays, etc. is just a total miracle. I am grateful for that. How about just the ability to pursue your dreams? You have the ability and so does everyone, but how many people are afraid to pursue the dream? Many!

Too many! What is stopping you?

Take a minute to think about those who are important in your life, and then tell them that you love them and care about them. Be thankful for what you have. You may wake up one day and have a piece of it missing.

APPRECIATE YOUR PARENTS AND LOVED ONES

I ask you this question: "If someone you loved was given less than 30 days to live and you could say anything to that person; What would you say? Who would that person be? Why havn't you done it?

How many times have you complained that your parents or guardians are getting on your case or being too nosey? Have you ever said you can't stand them and can't wait until you no longer live in their house?

Think about something. Why do you think that they wait up for you when you're out late? Why do they tell you to be home at a certain time? It's not because they're on your case. It's because they love and care about you.

The next time your parents or guardians are waiting up for you or tell you to be home at a certain time, thank them. Tell them that you appreciate the fact that they care enough about you to worry.

I have never met one person in my entire life who doesn't want to be cared for and loved. Imagine if no one cared. Many teenagers in the world don't have loving parents or guardians. Many teenagers are beaten daily, sexually abused, and physically and emotionally scarred for life.

Appreciate your parents and loved ones. Tell them that you love, respect, and care about them. The problem with most teenagers is that they take their parents and those who care about them for granted. They don't realize what their loved ones may have sacrificed and done for them throughout the years.

What The People Are Asking:

 If you could send one message to a kid who has lost a parent what would that message be?

- Britanni D., Parent of a Student, Versailles, OH

Answer: I am sorry! It'll be ok. Life may not be fair, but we all have things we have to accept and deal with. This is what you have to accept and deal with. Allow yourself to grieve, but the reality is we have to move on and live our lives. I'm not saying you ever forget that parent, but you put up pictures and you live your best life and know that that parent is looking down on you and wants you to be happy and wants to be proud of you. Live your best life!

Remember also, that you lost a parent. People lose parents every day. I know this doesn't make it any easier, but remember no matter how bad you have it some people have it worse.

I have a friend. A dear friend whose name is Eileen and she lost a son. I'll never forget the day that JoJo died. The call came into my office and shocked us all. JoJo was five years old and died in his sleep. Can you imagine? She had to bury a child.

This might not make it any easier, but remember, no matter what we have to deal with, there are people that have it thousands times worse. Eileen is one of my heroes and a woman that I have the utmost respect for.

 Why do parents getting divorced make high school so hard for us teens?
- *Tyler V., Union Endicott High School, NY*

Answer: I don't think it is parents getting divorced that make high school so hard. It is the situation that you are dealing with that makes concentrating and enjoying high school so hard. Listen, I know it is hard and painful because now there are a lot of unknowns in your life. This is tough, but would you rather your parents be together just for the kids and their happiness? That isn't healthy, nor would you want that. This isn't about you and you shouldn't take sides. Concentrate on your school and your life and give this time for your questions to be answered.

Stop reading this book now. Don't read any further today. Just put the book away and sit back and think about all the little things that your loved ones have sacrificed for you. How have they gone out of their way to help you? Show them you appreciate them by telling them "thank you" and that you love them. Do it now. You never know what may happen tomorrow. They may not be around.

CHAPTER TWELVE

THE CONCLUSION OF A GREAT LIFE

My life today is rich with love and made meaningful through the support and testimonials from people who have heard my message. My life is fulfilling, challenging, rewarding, and a journey of happiness and giving. I have the greatest job in the world. Every year more than one million students and teachers hear and benefit from my message.

I have a beautiful wife, Marsha, who has been there with love, support, encouragement, and sanity. Along with my wife, I have many friends and family members who are incredibly dear to me. To me that is special. I couldn't be who I am today if it weren't for the support and love of those around me. I am so thankful to all the people who have been there along the way and have helped me reach the position I am in now. I have realized one cannot do it alone.

If you invest in helping others reach their dreams, then people will invest in helping you reach yours. That may have taken me time to learn but, as I have learned, it was well worth the wait in the end. All my life I wanted to be successful. Not really knowing what success was, I just wanted it. It was all about me and what I wanted: money and financial freedom. I knew exactly what I wanted to earn in terms of dollars, the house I would live in, and the car I would drive. I wanted to make a nice living. What is a nice living? I can tell you this, ladies and gentleman: The moment my attitude changed and I was less concerned with making a living and I started to concentrate more on making a difference, I made a much more significant living.

THE JOURNEY IS WHAT WE MISS, BUT IT'S WHAT LIFE IS REALLY ABOUT

Success is the journey and not the destination. One's true success is the significance felt when helping other people achieve what they want in life. Significance is a personal feeling of living a life that has made a difference in the lives of other people. I wish you many titles and testimonials throughout your life, but I am sure you will find true satisfaction comes from testimonies rather than titles.

I am successful because I am on a journey that I have set and created. I am doing what I love and journeying toward my goals and dreams. I am significant because I am reaching out to help others by making them feel special and good about themselves. I receive letters and emails from those who have really been touched by my words. Those letters and emails are testimonies of my significance.

I think significance is far more important than financial success. I really think it is about helping others before helping oneself. I wish you greatness in life and lots of titles, successes, testimonies, and significance. However, if you had to choose among them, go for testimonies and significance. If you do, you will find life to be extremely rewarding and fulfilling, meaningful, and significant. Good luck, and God Bless.

I personally hope that you have enjoyed reading this book as much as I have enjoyed writing it for you. Bye!

What The Students Are Asking:

 If you could change something in the world what would it be?
- *Bryan P., Rockwood High School, PA*

Answer: I wish that I could change children with disabilities such as down syndrome or autism. I have a nephew, Patrick, that is 19 years old and it saddens me the way people treat him. Patrick knows that he isn't normal and that he'll never lead a normal life, but he wishes he could. All he wants is a girlfriend, to go to a teenage party, and to be normal. I wish Patrick and all others children with disabilities didn't have to suffer and know that they are different. I wish we didn't have differences in the world and that was a cure.

 What's the best thing to do if bullied, and how do we not let bullying affect us?
- *Adrian H, Australia*

Answer: This is going to be short because the answer doesn't require any more words than the words I am going to use to answer your question. The best thing to do when being bullied is to just ignore the person or people. Ignore them! Don't let bullying affect you by not giving the people the power to have an affect on how you feel about yourself. Like really?!?!?! Who are they? Ignore them and don't let them rule your emotions.

THE LAST WORD

One of the greatest things we can do in the world is learning to help others. It is the best feeling in the world to know that you have made a difference in someone's life by helping them. That's what the world and our society should be about, helping others, especially the less fortunate.

I have listed here what I think are some things you should keep in mind in order to be a good person:

- Listen more than you talk.
- Be on time.
- Be grateful.
- Help others without expecting anything in return.
- Express your interest in others.
- Be honest.
- Open the door for other people.
- Say hello with a smile.
- Put other people's needs before your own needs.
- And respect all people, even your annoying sister.

ABOUT THE AUTHOR

Jeff Yalden is one of the most sought-after youth speakers in all of North America. He has addressed hundreds of youth conferences, and thousands of middle schools, high schools, colleges, and universities. His wisdom and unparalleled ability to reach into the hearts of his audience have enabled him to share his message with audiences in all 50 states and to audiences representing over 48 different countries. Since 1995, Jeff has been speaking professionally and has addressed more than four million teens and educators.

He was a distinguished member of the National Speakers Association, International Speakers Association, and New England Speakers Association. Jeff has earned the designation of Certified Speaking Professional, a designation earned by fewer than 7 percent of all professional speakers worldwide. Along with his success speaking, Jeff was also two-time Marine of the Year and Mr. New Hampshire Male America.

In addition to his current book, Jeff is the author of "They Call Me Coach", "Keep It Simple: A Teenagers Handbook for Life!" "20 Ways to Keep It Simple", "Traits of a Leader" and "Pathway to Purpose." He is the co-author of "Lead Now – or Step Aside!" and contributing author to the New York Times #1 bestseller, "A Cup of Chicken Soup for the Soul."

From his past to his present, Jeff has lived his message, making it more real and entertaining. As a student in high school, Jeff graduated 128th out of 133 students. He was rejected by 16 of the 19 colleges to which he applied. Having grown up with a learning disability, stutter, ADD, and ADHD, Jeff had to struggle and fight hard to overcome obstacles.

When Jeff is not on the road inspiring young and old alike, he resides in Cape Cod, Mass. with his wife Marsha and their fish named Bo, Nemo, and 23 fish and counting, all named Cocoa.

Jeff enjoys riding his Harley Davidson motorcycle and spending time with family and friends on his boat, "The Motivator!"

Nothing makes Jeff more proud than the time he spends with his nieces and nephews and watching them grow up. Jeff loves being Uncle Jeff and being THAT crazy Uncle.

What The Students Are Asking:

 What is your favorite part about being a motivational speaker?
- Cooper N., Quincy High School, IL

Answer: My favorite part of being a motivational speaker is giving people what I wish someone had given me. I love the fact that I am able to share my story and life in a way that teens and my audiences can appreciate. I'm just honored and blessed to do what I love and speaking to youth audiences is what I really love to do.

 What is the most rewarding experience you have had about speaking to schools?
– Ryan R., Ocean Township High School, NJ

Answer: The most rewarding experience is that what I say makes sense and people remember me long after I have left the building. I can literally walk through a mall and nearly every time I am stopped by someone that has seen me speak or someone that has seen me on television. I love that my message resonates with my audiences. It's an incredible feeling to know I am making my mark on the world.

 What is the most emotional speech you have ever heard or given?

- Cam G., Burrillville High School, RI

Answer: The most emotional speech I have personally given was the day after I lost my dog, Chase. I didn't want to speak, but I wanted to speak. It was tough, but I'd never been so present in my talk. Jimmy Valvano's "Don't Give Up" speech at the ESPN ESPY Awards in March of 1992 was the greatest motivational talk I have ever listened to. This talk started the Jimmy V Foundation to raise money for cancer research. I would encourage you to google "Jimmy V Don't Give Up" and listen to his 11-minute talk. It is simply the greatest motivational talk I have ever listened to. In fact, I still listen to it quite often.

 What inspired you to become a inspirational/motivational speaker?

- Brandon S., Mahwah High School, NJ

Answer: My past and what I've been through. I wanted to share with others so they didn't have to feel as inadequate as I did. I'm so glad this is the path and journey I took. It's been incredible and has made everything I've been through so worth all the hurt and pain.

CONTACT JEFF
TODAY FOR YOUR NEXT
YOUTH EVENT

Programs are available for:

Middle Schools

High Schools

Colleges

Universities

Youth Leadership Conferences

Church Programs

Teacher In-Services

Parent/Community Programs

Corporate Events

Commencement Addresses

For information about Jeff

and his programs please visit:

www.JeffYalden.com

or call today

Toll Free 1-800-948-9289

QUICK ORDER FORM

Call: (800) 948-9289
Web: www.jeffyalden.com
Write: Jeff Yalden
122 Pheasant Run Drive, Murrells Inlet, SC 29576

Please send me copies of **"Your Life Matters"** at $12.95 each, plus shipping and handling.

Name: _____ Date: _____

Address: _____

City: _____ State: _____ Zip: _____

Phone: _____

Email: _____

Shipping: US: $3 for the first book and $2 for each additional book.
International: Based on ship-to location and current rates; please call for exact amounts.

Payment type: ☐ Credit Card ☐ Check/Money Order ☐ Visa
☐ Mastercard ☐ American Express

Credit card #: _____

Name on card: _____ exp date: _____

Signature: _____

Made in the USA
Columbia, SC
02 February 2025

53133421R00085